IN PRAISE OF *A VOICE BEYOND WEEPING*

A Voice Beyond Weeping is a spellbinding account of survival in a family, which proves to all of us that no matter how serene things may seem on the surface, there may be a veritable cauldron bubbling underneath. I think this is going to be a must-read for any student of family dynamics, and it certainly is going to be an enlightening book for any layman.

Ferrol Sams, M.D., author of *Run with the Horsemen, The Whisper of the River, When All the World Was Young, The Widow's Mite*

A Voice Beyond Weeping is emotionally moving. The players are fascinating and complex. As I read, hardly able to put the book down, I laughed and cried with them as they made mistakes and grew and suffered and died and passed to others their legacy. Roberta Damon shares these wonderful people with her readers, and in the process, the characters in the book become family to the audience. The author has a powerful and charming way with words.

Ron Dubois, PhD, Family Therapist

T0095974

Only Roberta Damon could write so eloquently about three mothers—her own! The book sings the melody of compassion, orchestrated by wisdom and tenacity. Dr. Damon is a marvelous technician of the English language. Her expressive syntactical prose stimulates the literary imagination. I recommend to those who need a sanctum sanctorum for processing their own family histories this reflective narrative, A Voice Beyond Weeping.

William David Kirkpatrick, PhD, Professor of Theology

Roberta Damon's A Voice Beyond Weeping *was scribed out of need to put down the words to tell us of her three mothers for ordering her own life script, as opposed to screenplays and novels written with the audience or readers in mind. She should have died! What makes an infant keep crying indefinitely to stay alive versus one that suffers a marasmic unresponsive and expressionless death? All readers will be able to empathize and identify with "Bertie," but if you are an "Okie." or any midwesterner, and Protestant churchgoing was a part of your upbringing, you will especially relate to this book.*

John E. Poarch, M.D., author of *LIMITS: The Keystone of Emotional Growth,* and *I Want It All*

Roberta M. Damon

A Voice
Beyond Weeping

A MEMOIR

ROBERTA M. DAMON

A VOICE BEYOND WEEPING

A MEMOIR

Oviedo, Florida

A Voice Beyond Weeping: A Memoir
by Roberta M. Damon

Copyright © 2018 by Roberta Damon. All rights reserved.

Published by HigherLife Development Services, Inc.
PO Box 623307
Oviedo, Florida 32762
(407) 563-4806
www.ahigherlife.com

Print: 978-1-7325026-2-8
Ebook: 978-1-7325026-5-9

10 9 8 7 6 5 4 3 2

Printed in the United States of America

This book was originally published in 2002 by Greystone Press,
Gladys S. Lewis, editor and publisher.

Dedicated to the memory of my three mothers:
Keith, May, and Mary Lou

"A voice was heard in Ramah,

a lamentation, and bitter weeping:

It was Rachel weeping for her children...

because they were not."

Jeremiah 31:15

In shady green pastures so rich and so sweet,
God leads his dear children along.
Where the water rolls down at the weary one's feet,
God leads his dear children along.
Some through the water, some through the flood,
Some through the fire, but all through the blood.
Some through great trial, but God gives a song,
In the night season and all the day long.

FOREWORD

Who is Roberta Damon? She is all of the following—but not just these: She is a former career missionary, a Christian family counselor, a published poet, a charismatic pulpiteer, and a dynamic teacher. She is also daughter, sister, wife and mother. But she is more than the sum of these parts.

What is this AVBW? Primarily, it is Roberta's story of being a daughter, a sister, and a mother, lovingly remembered and framed through the wisdom she has developed through her lifelong experiences as a missionary, psychological counselor, and gifted wordsmith. In AVBW, Roberta displays not just her voice, but her eye for the telling detail, and her ear, finely-tuned for real and imagined dialogue, that matches the talents of John Grisham.

AVBW is all of the following, but more than these: It is a memoir of Roberta's Depression-era Oklahoma family of origin. It is also a fictionalized docu-biography. It is a moving meditation on the paradoxes of family love and hate, as it was played out in the fortunes of the older generations. The threads that weave the tapestry of her family's destinies are traced further as her narrative continues into the present day—as she and her adult siblings have come to new stages in their life journeys.

It is a journalistic recollection of her recent discoveries of some new truths concerning her father and her three mothers (and she means this literally). Roberta skillfully moves from past to present and back again. Now she shows us how things today came about from the flashbacks of her parents' courtship and marriage. Again, she shows us how today's tensions and dislocations in her nearest and dearest were painfully inevitable as consequences of the past.

Most miraculously, it is the story of how she found her "third mother" who she was certain had been lost long ago in her earliest childhood.

When you pick up this book, you will find it to be a gripping page-turner you won't want to put down. On one page Roberta has you in stitches, and on the next page, in tears. Pastors will want to quote the book in the pulpit. Scholars and professors will want to footnote it in their journal articles about therapy and family psychology.

Dedicated to her "three mothers," AVBW proves the axiom that, "Everybody has a family." Everyone has a family history—a set of family myths, lore, stories, and memories— that, for good or ill, forever casts the destiny and identity of every member. What a rare pleasure to read such a graceful, intimate, embracing look back to her roots.

David Thomas, Associate Professor of Rhetoric (retired) at the University of Richmond

TABLE OF CONTENTS

In the Beginning

They came from everywhere. They were possessed by a fever. They came in wagon trains or in single wagons drawn by oxen. They came on horseback, or afoot. They forsook all and followed the sun–West. They left father and mother and houses and lands and came to a new land which the Lord showed them. They built houses and dwelled therein. They planted gardens and ate the fruit of them. They took wives and begot sons and daughters and took wives for their sons. They gave their daughters to husbands that they might increase there and not diminish. They built cities and towns and sought the peace of the cities. They came with guns and Bibles. Neither drought, nor flood, nor sickness, nor height nor depth nor any other creature could dissuade them. They were the pioneers.

The first to arrive prepared the way for the others. They made straight the way. They made the rough places smooth. They beat a path across the wilderness. They left the depleted land of the Mississippi Delta, the worn out cotton fields of Georgia and Alabama. They left the mountains of Tennessee and the old disappointments of Virginia and the Carolinas. They turned their backs on the old and set their faces toward the new. They set out in spring and arrived in summer. They claimed their land and lived in soddies or boarded tents. They cleared the land and before winter they had built cabins. They faced heat and cold, hunger and isolation, ridicule and unending labor. Women died in childbirth and men grew old before their time. But they endured. These were the pioneers.

A wagon train came to a rickety bridge. The men dismounted to assess its strength. They had been traveling for weary weeks on what passed for a road–ruts cut by the wheels of the wagons that had gone before. As they approached the bridge, they saw a rustic sign that some earlier pioneer had nailed onto one of the supports. They moved closer so they could read the faded letters: "They said we couldn't do it, but we did." The words were murmured, then spoken and repeated until a great exultant shout erupted. What can stop us? "Shall tribulation or distress or persecution or famine or nakedness or peril or sword?" No! We are conquerors. These were the pioneers.

The land had belonged to the Caddos, Kiowas, Wichitas, Comanches, and Apaches. Now it belonged to those whose names were drawn in the lottery. The person whose name was drawn could claim a parcel of land–either acres for farming or a city lot. The new owner could farm it, build a house on it, or sell it to someone else. The place of their arrival was first called Lathram. Established as a town-site, almost overnight home sites and businesses sprang up. Incorporated in 1906, it was settled a year before President Theodore Roosevelt signed the proclamation declaring Oklahoma a state. But some other town was already called Lathram. The suggestion came that the town be named Carnegie after the great philanthropist. So, Carnegie it was–and is.

The town grew and prospered. The settlers built a city park. By 1912, they had built a hydroelectric power company which furnished electricity to forty-five customers. They added city water, a sewage treatment plant, and the Chamber of Commerce–in that order. They erected a flag pole in the center of town at the intersection of Main and Broadway where the well and watering trough used to be.

In 1922, the Junior class of Carnegie High School ended their history of their town with these words: "Reports from agents along the Rock Island show that Carnegie ships more farm produce than any other town on the Mangum branch—hence the slogan adopted by the Chamber of Commerce, 'The Busiest Town on the Rock Island.' Carnegie, with a population of fifteen hundred, has all the advantages of a modern city. Lights, power, sewers, water—all are here. The business streets are macadamized and oiled with crude oil. Some of the institutions which mark Carnegie as a more progressive town than its neighbors include four big grain elevators, two cotton gins, three banks, a flouring mill, a broom factory, bottling works, an ice plant, an ice cream factory, an elegantly furnished funeral home, and mercantile establishments second to none in the country. Carnegie is blessed with a live-wire, progressive, forward-looking citizenship."

Carnegie was a boom town—an alabaster city, set, not on a hill, but in the fertile valley of the Washita River.

WASHINGTON D.C.–MAY 1966

Mother sent me a copy of the publication from the United States Printing Office about daddy's hearing, a part of the Congressional Record. I eagerly opened it to see what was said about him. It was most impressive. The week before, President Lyndon Johnson had called my father into the Oval Office to tell him he was to receive a presidential nomination for an important post. My dad had been legislative assistant to Senator Robert Samuel Kerr of Oklahoma. In those days, Kerr was known as the "Uncrowned King of the Senate." My father had worked for him for many years. Dad was often called "the third senator from Oklahoma." He had hitched his wagon to Bob Kerr's star when the senator was governor. He had stayed all through the years Kerr was in the Senate.

They had been ardent Democratic warriors together during the Eisenhower administration, when the chances of getting an appropriations bill through Congress had been next to nil. Their aim was to bring water to their state, primarily through the development of the vast Arkansas River basin. When Kerr envisioned the Port of Catoosa, and ocean going barges on the Arkansas River, he was derided and called the "Admiral of the Arkansas." Something of that early pioneer claim persevered in his goals for his dream: "They said we couldn't do it, but we did." When Senator Kerr died on New Year's Day, 1963, something in my father died, also. In their heyday, when Lyndon Johnson was majority leader of the Senate, he and Bob Kerr were power brokers. My father was a part of that team. When Senator Kerr wrote his book about "land, wood, and water," daddy autographed my copy:

"Dear Bertie,
The Senator has said some nice things about your dad. Maybe you would like to read them. This book is the story of a team of which I am happy to be the 'bat boy.'
Dad"

I remember as a graduate student at the University of Maryland, I would sometimes hitch a ride with a friend into the Capitol, spend a couple of hours in the Library of Congress doing research, and then ride home to Alexandria with daddy. If he wasn't ready, I'd go up to the Senate chamber and watch Lyndon Johnson wheel and deal. It was an education. One day, as I was walking back over to the Senate Office Building from the Congressional Library, I realized that the Majority Leader was going my way. I was struck speechless in his presence.

He looked at me, smiled, and said, "We seem to be going the same direction." He must have known how flustered I was.

I swallowed and blurted, "I think you know my daddy. He works in Senator Kerr's office."

Johnson, tall and imposing, gave me his full and considerable attention. "Who is your daddy?"

"Don McBride."

"Oh, honey, I've known your daddy for years. We have done some mighty good work together." He asked me where and what I was studying and, consummate politician that he was, seemed to be genuinely interested when I told him I was working on a Master's degree in English literature.

When my father sat opposite him in the oval office, the President asked, "Don, whatever happened to your daughter who was working on a Master's degree at the University of Maryland?"

My father was astounded that he remembered that brief encounter. It was a trademark of Johnson's. My dad answered, "She and her husband are Baptist missionaries in South Brazil."

"Well, that's wonderful. We need more people like that in this country."

They chatted like the two old friends they were. Johnson had just announced he would not run for a second full term. My father reported afterwards that the President seemed lonely and eager to talk about the old days and the old conquests. They spoke of Bob Kerr, of course, and of Mike Monroney, at the time senior Senator from Oklahoma. Monroney had taken on some of Kerr's staff, including my father, but for my dad, it was never the same. Dad's loyalty had been to Bob Kerr. Now, the President of the United States was offering my father a directorship of the monolithic Tennessee Valley

Authority, a nine-year term. Dad was almost sixty-four years old. Such an appointment required a Senate confirmation. He was afraid he might be turned down because of his age. That was not the case.

The Committee on Public Works of the United States Senate convened May 17, 1966, in Room 4200 Senate Office Building, Senator Fred R. Harris of West Virginia presiding. I quickly scanned the information: Senators present: Harris, Randolph, Muskie, Gruening, Moss, Jordan, Inouye, Montoya, Tydings, Cooper, Fong, Boggs, and Pearson. I read on eagerly.

Senator Harris: "We have before the committee this morning the nomination of Mr. Don McBride to be a member of the Board of Directors of the Tennessee Valley Authority. Don McBride is well known to most of us on the committee. He served as special assistant to the late Senator Bob Kerr on water resources matters, and was instrumental in drafting much of the legislation relating to rivers and harbors and flood control that emanated from this committee during the period that Senator Kerr served as a Member of the Senate. He played an important role in drafting the Water Supply Act of 1958, which permits both the Corps of Engineers and the Bureau of Reclamation to incorporate the storage in reservoirs for low flow regulation and for municipal and industrial water supply. This law has proven to be of immense value in combating water shortages throughout the country. The President has made a wise selection in placing this nomination before the Senate. Without objection, I would like to place into the record at this point a biographical sketch of Don McBride, which reveals the executive and engineering background possessed by this man which I certainly feel highly qualifies him for this most important post."

Carl Albert, the Speaker of the House of Representatives, sang daddy's praises. Various senators gave glowing reports of dad's expertise, his courtesy, and his integrity. After hearing the accolades, Senator Gruening drew laughter from the committee. "It's hard to believe anybody could be that good," he said.

The biographical sketch included dad's early professional and personal history, as well as the long list of honors which had been heaped upon him during an illustrious career in public service. Although I did not know it at the time, some key personal history had been omitted. Years later, when I had occasion to reflect on our lives, I wondered how he managed to get through the FBI background check—not that he had committed any felonious act. He simply had some secrets that remained hidden—to the public, certainly, but also to his family. It was in an era when J. Edgar Hoover and his agents routinely collected the personal and often the sexual histories of men in order to destroy them.

I was proud of my father and his accomplishments. He ran on nervous energy that was translated into work. As far back as I can remember, he was driven to succeed. When I was a child, I thought daddy just wanted to get out of the house. It seemed to me he was always gone, always doing important things. He worked for the governor. As an adult, I have wondered if he drove himself to atone for his early sins. I imagine he was sweating out the FBI background check. But, this is not my father's story. This is the story of my three mothers.

MISSISSIPPI–1918

Her sweet face and gentle manner melted the hearts of various neighborhood swains, but when Melford Anderson came to call, May knew he was the one. May was loved by everyone who knew her. If there ever was anyone deserving of love, it was May. She looked at life and smiled, and life smiled back. "Good as gold" was what people said about May.

She lived in a time of cataclysmic events. The great World War was drawing to its conclusion. The Kaiser would soon be forced to sign the armistice. World leaders were engaged in great debates, but this fifteen-year-old girl from McComb, Mississippi, was not one whit interested in world events. She was interested in Melford Anderson.

Melford was solid. He was built square, and his feet were steadfastly planted in reality. He was a pragmatist with a warm heart. When he laughed, his plain face lighted with merriment. Melford discovered early that he was not afraid of hard work. "Salt of the earth" was what folks said of him.

Melford took his time about courting. If truth be told, he took his time about most everything he did. Melford was a plodder. He thought things through. Once he had made up his mind, he pretty well stayed convinced. When he knew he loved May, he concocted a plan. He would ask her to marry him. If she said no, he would go out west and be a bachelor for the rest of his life. If she said yes, he'd take her with him and raise a family. He thought it unnecessary to get down on one knee. They sat on her father's front porch swing in the soft Mississippi summer night.

"In Oklahoma things are booming. We could get us some land. Everybody's building out there. They need carpenters. We could build ourselves a house, too. And we could fill it up with kids. How does that sound to you?" He was almost sure what her answer would be. Almost.

May slipped her small hand into his large already calloused

one, and in a voice firm with conviction, she gave him the answer he wanted. "If you're going to Oklahoma, Melford Anderson, I'm going with you." She paused for a moment. "Well, aren't you going to kiss me?"

Melford obliged, found he liked it, and kissed her again. Then he grinned. "Let's go talk to your daddy."

And so it was that, a few months later, May stood with Melford in her parents' parlor and promised to love, honor, and obey him. It was a promise he never gave her reason to regret. They were young. They had their entire lives ahead of them. In 1920, people were old at fifty. Life expectancy was not much above that. May beat all the odds. Of course, they had no way of knowing what lay ahead when, that next spring they packed up all they owned. With the energy of youth and great optimism, they headed west to what, a few short years before, had been Indian Territory. Rogers and Hammerstein might well have had May and Melford in mind when they wrote their musical so many years later:

"They couldn't pick a better time to start in life.

It ain't too early and it ain't too late.

Starting as a farmer with a brand new wife,

Soon be living in a brand new state,

Brand new state,

Gonna treat you greeeaaaaat!

OOOOOOOOklahoma where the wind comes sweeping down the plain. . ."

CARNEGIE—1922

They made a garden. Melford cleared and plowed the acre. Together, he and May planted it and tended it. They prayed for rain. And the rains came. In a few weeks, green fuzz appeared down the straight rows. May and Melford stood at the edge of the garden in the evening arm-in-arm, tired from their day's work, but proud of what their work was producing. Corn and beans, potatoes and onions, okra and tomatoes, butterbeans and black eyed peas appeared in embryonic form. In spite of her thickening middle, May worked her garden in the mornings before the sun sent her indoors. In turn, she hoed and weeded. From mid-June until the end of July, she picked, washed, cooked, canned, and stored the bounty. The labor involved was unremitting. It was, however, not optional. They lived on what they could produce.

Adjacent to their garden was their house, built with their own hands. Melford was a carpenter. He knew the language of plumb lines, levels, and planes. He followed the rule to measure twice and cut once. His eye was accurate and his judgment sure. The sawdust drifted down from the gash the saw blade cut into the two-by-fours. It fell into a pile beneath the sawhorses. The steady *shoom-shoom-shoom* was a rhythmic song produced by muscle, sinew, and sweat, and when Melford picked up his plane to smooth the pine boards, curls of a delicate butter hue fell softly to the ground. The house rose on its solid foundation, a testimony to the faith, that without work, is dead.

May was in her mid-teens. Melford was ten years her senior. In her eyes, he was everything a man ought to be—protector, provider, fount of all wisdom, kind companion, and spiritual guide. At twenty-six, Melford was a man who had already accomplished much. He had taken a bride, brought her to this place, acquired land, built their house, found employment, and done his part to ensure that the Anderson name would not be blotted from the book of life. May was not afraid with Melford by her side. He felt deeply the responsibility that comes with being husband and father.

In early September, May awoke to a dull pain in her lower back. At first, she was not particularly alarmed. She was largely ignorant of the birth process, but she had picked up bits and pieces of information along the way. Female friends and neighbors got together to sew or quilt. Whenever there were two or three married women in a group, the discussion inevitably turned to a comparison of labor pains. These discussions took place among women experienced in such things. Single women were excluded by reason of decency. Men were certainly excluded, because nice women didn't discuss such things with men—not even the men who were the cause of the labor pains.

May had heard that first babies often take their time getting born. As she lay on her side in her bed, her belly huge and distended, her ankles and feet swollen, she tried not to think of the pain. She tried to think good thoughts. She remembered a sermon their pastor had preached about motherhood. He had said that mothers were true heroes. May didn't feel particularly heroic. In fact, she was aware of a flicker of fear that nagged beneath the good thoughts. She felt very young and far from her mother. The preacher had said that when women give birth, they descend into the valley of the shadow of death. May's mind veered toward Psalm twenty-three: "Though I walk through the valley of the shadow of death, I will fear no evil for Thou art with me." The preacher said that mothers pluck the roses from their own cheeks and plant them in the rosy faces of their husbands' babies. As May recalled, that sermon had made every man in the congregation squirm in discomfort. She felt her first hard contraction.

May had a close call in the valley of the shadow. She very

nearly died giving birth to their son. During the hard labor, Melford paced from one end of the house to the other. He would stay by May as long as he could stand it, and then he would have to leave the cramped little bedroom. His hands were bruised from her hard grasp. Never had he seen such pain. Never had he seen so much blood. The women who attended the birthing wiped her sweating face with a damp rag. They rubbed her feet and neck and back. They assured her with words and with their presence. They drank gallons of strong, black coffee. After May had labored for two days and two nights, she and everyone in the house with her were exhausted. Then, they called in Doc Parsons. May was conscious only of the red pain and the voices that kept insisting: "Push. Push. Push. Push." With one mighty convulsive effort, the baby's head emerged. Then the rest of him slid into the world and into the waiting arms of his trembling father. May's flesh was badly torn. The baby was a big, healthy, squalling boy—red-faced and kicking. The women bathed him and attended to May. They cleaned up the mess, wiped her down with a cool, damp cloth, and put a clean gown on her. They brushed her damp hair and smoothed her brow. They expertly changed the sheets beneath her, and put a fresh pillow under her head. Then, they placed her newborn in her arms. She looked at him in wonder and was convinced he was the most beautiful thing she had ever seen. He eagerly nursed at her breast while she counted his fingers and toes and marveled at the head full of dark hair. May looked like a child holding a baby doll. Melford thought he had never seen her more beautiful. He thought of the Madonna.

She looked up at Melford, "I've decided. I'm naming him Charles after my daddy."

"Charles is a good name. It's a strong name. Our son is

named after a good man." Melford took the baby from her arms, and May fell into an exhausted slumber. The young father sat in the rocking chair with the baby in his arms. He stared at his son. Charles was unimpressed. He yawned.

"Welcome to the world, Charles Anderson," his daddy whispered.

Dr. Parsons, looking grim, stepped into the living room. "Now, Melford, I know your wife says she wants a houseful of children, but you listen to me. If you don't want to lose her, you will see to it that she does not have another child. She will die the next time. You be careful. Do you understand what I'm saying to you?"

"Yeah, I understand. My God, Doc. I'll never forget this. I'll never put her through this again. But it's going to break her heart not to have more children."

"Better a broken heart than a dead wife and an orphaned son. That little boy needs his mama. Now, you just be damn good and careful with her. You hear me?"

Melford nodded. "If anything happened to her, I don't know what I'd do."

"Well, there's one thing you can't do, and that's get her pregnant again." Doc Parsons dried his hands on a kitchen towel and packed his black bag. "I'll be back in the morning to check on her."

May cried when he told her. He knew she would. He held her clumsily and wiped her tears. "It's going to be okay, May. I don't want anything bad to happen to you. We've got a boy who needs you. And I need you, too. If the Lord only sends us this one child, why, we got to be grateful."

"I am grateful. I just wanted him to have lots of brothers and sisters."

"I know that, but I'd rather he have a mother."

So May poured out all her considerable love on Charles, and he blossomed under her nurturing care.

It was a good life. Melford was a carpenter, a builder, a night watchman, and a farmer—a jack-of-all-trades and master of them all. If anything needed fixing, Melford could fix it. If there was a job to be done, he could do it. And May worked right along beside him.

Melford was not a man of letters, but he knew the Bible. He thought that the thirty-first chapter of Proverbs was written about May: "The heart of her husband doth safely trust in her." (Melford nodded and thought how much he trusted May.) "She will do him good and not evil all the days of her life." (He agreed.) "She worketh willingly with her hands." (He thought, "Now that's May all over again. She does work hard.") "Strength and honor are her clothing." ("May is a little bitty thing, but she's tough. And honor? Why she couldn't do a dishonorable thing if she tried.") "In her tongue is the law of kindness." ("There's no one sweeter than May on this earth.") "She looketh well to the ways of her household, and eateth not the bread of idleness." ("There's not a lazy bone in her body. She suits me just fine.")

Melford never tired of watching May and their infant son. She nursed the baby in the rocking chair that had belonged to his grandmother. They had brought it with them when they came to Oklahoma from Mississippi. May and Charles, mother and son. They were the picture of contentment. Melford thought, "I am one lucky S.O.B."

Theirs was a good marriage. Neither May nor Melford had the disposition or the desire for argument. Neither had a need to win or to control. Theirs was a cooperative effort. They decided early that if there were problems, they would sit down at the kitchen table with a cup of coffee and talk until the problems were solved. It seemed the sensible thing to do. As Charles grew, he took his place at the table with them and became a participating member of the family. May described her husband as "jolly." Melford described her as "the best thing that ever happened to me." Charles knew at an early age that he was a lucky kid.

South Carolina/Texas Oklahoma–1879-1925

Malcolm McGregor was born in South Carolina. As a young man, he heeded Horace Greeley's admonition to "go west, young man, go west." He did go west–all the way to Texas. He married Nettie Hensley, a Texas girl, born and bred. Their son, Royden Keith, was born in 1879. Everyone called him R.K. from the time he was little. He grew up around tools and mules and served his time behind a plow. Like all boys growing up in that raw, new land, he worked with his hands and was no stranger to hammer and saw. When R.K. was full grown, he worked for a time on the Santa Fe Railroad as fireman and engineer. He was not quite twenty-four when, on Christmas eve, he married Effie Alma Lee. In spite of their best efforts over the years, they had no sons. Keith was the second of their three daughters, named, of course, for her daddy.

"Who ever heard of a girl named Keith?" R.K. picked up his newest daughter. He was pleased that Effie wanted to name her after him.

"Who ever heard of a girl named Orvilla?" Effie patted her first born on the head. "Now we have two beautiful daughters, and they both have beautiful names."

Effie was prone to female complaints–headaches, monthly discomfort, and delicate nerves. She doctored herself regularly with Lydia Pinkham's Compound and hot camomile tea. She stayed in bed in a darkened room with a cold cloth on her head as often as she could manage it. Effie didn't plan on having any more children. Sexual intercourse was a foolish and inconvenient duty; pregnancy was dreadful, and childbirth infinitely worse. R.K. did the cooking and cleaning, and he kept his daughters quiet so their mother could rest.

R.K. and Effie were Baptists, but of the two, Effie was the religious one. She found great comfort in reading scripture, and when she prayed, the Lord heard. He did not always answer, but Effie expected Him to. R.K., on the other hand, lived in the world of Texas railroad men. He could cuss with the best of them–or the worst. It was not until he was approaching middle age that he felt called to preach and to become a missionary. At thirty-seven, R.K. gave up cussing, packed up his wife and his little girls, and moved to Chickasha, Oklahoma. By that time, like it or not, Effie had given birth to Annie Laurie, their third daughter. Effie stayed home and coped while R.K. served the new churches in the Chickasha Baptist Association as an associational missionary. It was 1916. Oklahoma was ten years old–the same age as Keith.

So, Keith grew up as a preacher's kid. Being a PK was not bad, but it was something like growing up in a fish bowl. Everyone was interested in how Effie and R.K. lived their lives and reared their children. Mostly, people were idly curious with no malicious intent. There were those in the congregation who kept track of the McGregor girls' sins and shortcomings. The sins of the three little girls, however, were remarkably few and not particularly interesting. Orvilla might sass her mama, or stamp her foot in anger. The baby, Annie Laurie, was too young to sin, and Keith was a compliant child. By and large, the family was admired. Keith, the pleaser, was universally loved. Blessed with a sunny disposition, she basked and blossomed in the approval of her father's flock. Their approbation was like food and water to her. Her life, enjoyable and uncomplicated, was filled with church picnics, watermelon cuttings, school projects, family visits, hay rides, pallets on the floor, all day singing and dinner on the grounds. Hers was a life of friendships and laughter. No doubt about it, Keith McGregor was Sunday's child.

When she graduated from Chickasha High School, Keith went to college. She didn't have far to go. Oklahoma College for Women was right there in Chickasha, within walking distance of the parsonage. Keith joined the student body with alacrity. She lived at home, but that didn't keep her from participating in college activities. Her photo albums were soon filled to overflowing with pictures of her and her girl friends at the swimming pool, in front of the library, in the 'Alice in Wonderland' costumes for Fall Festival. Keith was the White Rabbit.

Her life at college brimmed with fun and friendship, as well as serious study. Keith was a bright girl and a disciplined student. She studied bookkeeping, because it seemed a practical thing to do. Secretly, Keith dreamed of love, a husband and children, but she convinced herself that such were for some distant time. First, she wanted to make her mark. It was beginning to be fashionable for young women to talk of independence, of earning their own way. Women were coming into their own. Amelia Earhart was every young woman's hero. The students at OCW adopted her hairstyle as their own, wore loose fitting blouses, tight fitting pants, and aviator jackets. They vowed to each other that there was more to life than getting married and having some man's babies. But they did love male attention.

Keith had completed two years of college when her dad was called to pastor First Baptist Church of Carnegie. After almost ten years of being an itinerant preacher, encourager, and trouble shooter for the scattered churches in the Chickasha Association, R.K. settled down to pastor one church. He assumed his new duties on Feburary 1, 1925. Keith packed her books and her clothes, quit school, and moved with her parents. In Carnegie, she began her new life. She looked around for a job and was hired as a bookkeeper at Kelly Ford. Then she met Don.

CARNEGIE-1925

The following summer, one day in June, Charles and May sat on their back steps snapping green beans for canning. They'd had rain and the garden was coming in fast. May was only twenty three, but she had been a wife for seven years and a mother for six. In her short life, she had acquired all the skills necessary to the production of food and to the rearing of a child. The family ate out of the garden all summer: corn and beans, tomatoes and okra, squash, beets, and butterbeans. She canned what they would eat all winter. And when the jars were stored on the shelves in the cellar, they looked like jewels of gold and jade and ruby.

"Now honey, be careful to get the strings off good. We don't like to eat the strings."

"Okay, Mama." Charles had early acquired the attitude

toward work that his parents displayed. He had been helping with chores since he could walk, and took pride in his parents' approval of him. Never was there a child more loved than Charles Anderson. Never was there a child more loving. His brows knitted in concentrating effort as he snapped the beans and pulled off the strings from the ridged edges.

They heard Brother Mac's Model T backfire before they could see him coming around the bend in the dusty road. The car stopped with a shudder and one last blast. R.K. got out and walked toward them, smiling.

"Mornin,' Miz Anderson. Mornin' Charles."

"Mornin,' pastor." She smoothed her hair and her apron and stood to receive her guest. "Won't you come in and have a cup of coffee. It won't take a minute."

"No, thank you kindly." He had pulled a magazine from the front seat of his Ford.

"I just came to bring you this quarterly. You are going to teach junior boys in Sunday School. This quarterly has the Bible lessons."

"Why, Brother Mac, I can't do that. I've never taught before." Her eyes grew big and she felt her heart beat fast at the thought of all those wiggly little boys. "I just don't think I can do that."

"Yes, you can. You've got your Bible. You've got this quarterly and you've got God. That's all you need. You'll start on Sunday." With a wave, he climbed into his faithful Tin Lizzie, and was gone, relieved to have enlisted a teacher for the class no one else wanted to teach. May looked at the quarterly feeling unworthy and inadequate. What an awesome responsibility. Could she do it? "Well," she thought, "I've got my Bible. I've got my quarterly. And I've got God. I guess I can give it a try."

The next Sunday, R.K. stepped behind the pulpit. He looked across the congregation and pondered. While he preached his sermon, other thoughts intruded.

"God so loved the world. What does that mean?" *What's happening here? All I see are women and their kids.*

"It means that God's love is for everyone. God didn't just love white people, or rich people, or powerful people. God loves all people." *There's not a man in this congregation. Where are all the men?*

"It also means that God loves you. God loves people individually. While he loves the whole world, God also loves you, and he knows your name." *I'll ask someone after church where the men are. They ought to be in church.*

"If you do not know the love of God, if you do not know Jesus Christ as your personal Savior, you can open your heart today and accept His love. You can have life abundant here and life eternal in heaven. Come to Jesus today. Our invitation hymn is number 189. Let us stand as we sing 'Just As I Am Without One Plea.'" *I'll ask Miz Watson where Harry is. He ought to be in worship.*

After two junior boys had walked the aisle and professed their faith in Christ, and the congregation had voted to receive them for believer's baptism, R.K. pronounced the benediction and walked up the aisle to the front door of the church to shake hands with the folks as they left.

"That was a good sermon, pastor."

"I enjoyed your message this morning, pastor."

"You just did my heart good today, pastor."

R.K. smiled, shook hands with them all, and patted children on the head. Bernice Watson was one of the last to leave. The pastor stopped her. "Miz Watson, I was wondering this morning about Harry. Is he feeling poorly?"

"Oh, no, Brother Mac, he's fine."

"I haven't seen him in church for some time. As a matter of fact, I haven't seen any of the men in church for some time."

Bernice Watson blushed and ducked her head. "These are hard times, Brother Mac. The men aren't here because they're ashamed to come. They don't have fine clothes to wear. Well, neither do the women, but we come on, you know? But the men, well, all they have is their overalls, and they can't come to church in their overalls." She was near tears.

R.K. patted her hand. "You tell those men to come on. You tell them to wear their overalls, because I'll be wearing mine."

"You won't."

"Oh yes, I will. Now you tell them." He knew she would spread the word.

The next Sunday morning there were men in the congregation, each wearing overalls–faded, mended, and clean. And their pastor stood and preached in his overalls. He preached God's word where it says that "man looketh on the outward appearance, but God looketh on the heart." Sunday after Sunday, until times were better, R.K. McGregor preached in his overalls. And the men and women and children came to worship. Oh, how they loved their pastor.

CARNEGIE–1993

Your granddaddy was my pastor. He came by one morning and told me I was going to teach junior boys. I didn't think I could do it, but I've been working with children in church for sixty-seven years. All children need is love. Oh, honey, your grandmother was the best Christian I ever knew. She used to go over to the church basement and study her Bible and pray. She'd pray out loud. I asked her one day if I could just slip in and listen to her pray. I told her I wouldn't be any bother. Of course, she said that would be all right, and so I did. Soon other young women wanted to come to hear her, too, so she started a class. I finished the whole course on the Bible. Oh, she was a good teacher. I studied hard and I got a perfect score on the test at the end." She nodded her head pertly. "Yessir, a perfect score."

We sat in May's living room. Her quavering voice grew stronger when she talked about Brother and Mrs. McGregor. "Your grandfather always wanted one of his children or grandchildren to be a missionary. I never knew what happened to you. He would be so proud to know that you were a missionary in Brazil.

Kansas–1923

Don was dirty and hot and sweaty from the day's work. He and his brother, Shep, had already spent a week at wheat harvest. They were down from Nebraska, and like many young men, they planned their summer following the harvest. The work was hard, but the money was good. Don brushed straw from his neck and shoulders. Every muscle in his body ached. His back, neck, and arms were burned by the sun. He was a town kid. Even though he was a hustler, he was unaccustomed to sustained manual labor. Now he was headed to the Brubakers where he and Shep were boarding for the summer. All he wanted to do was stand under a cold shower and let the dirt and sweat roll off. And he was hungry. Mrs. Brubaker always had a table loaded down with good food.

Since he had arrived in Bird City, he had not been without a social life. He and Shep hung around with some of the other boys in for harvesting. One of the first things they did when they came to a new town was to check out the girls. It was the custom to see which fellow could get a town girl to drink a coke with him at the fountain in the town drugstore. And the girls were flattered by the attention. Maybe tonight, after they cleaned up and ate supper they would head for town. Maybe he would see that cute little blonde again. He didn't know her name yet, but someone said her daddy owned the bank in town. His heart lifted at the thought of getting to know her. It became obvious that other parts of his anatomy lifted as well.

Don did get to know her. She was pretty, sweet, and giddy. She was sixteen and thrilled at the hot attention from an older man. He was twenty and knew better. When he told her he loved her, she believed him. By early July, he had taken her behind the barn. By late August, she was sure she was pregnant. She went from giddy to scared. Her name was Bernice. Her family called her Bea. Her father was a man of considerable influence in that town. And she had three large, very strong older brothers—grown men with families of their own. They had been her fierce protectors since her birth.

When Bernice tearfully confessed her predicament to her mother, that lady, horrified and weeping, managed by euphemism and innuendo, to tell her husband. He let out a roar that could be heard on the other side of town. The men of the family met to decide between homicide and matrimony. They reluctantly decided on a shot gun wedding—a wedding that was hardly worthy of the name.

"We want you to understand that you will never touch our sister again. This wedding is for one purpose only, and that is to give her child a name. We will arrange for a divorce as soon as the baby is born." Her oldest brother looked serious.

"And you get your stinking carcass out of this town as soon as you've said 'I do.' We don't ever want to see you around here again." Her youngest brother looked fierce.

"My daughter is sixteen years old." Her father spoke with barely contained fury. "She's the one that has to live here. We're the ones who can't hold our heads up in this town. For God's sake. You have ruined my daughter. You have ruined her reputation. You have stolen her innocence. You're lucky we don't shoot you for this."

Don stood, ashen faced, on shaking legs and heard, as from a distance, the words of the wedding ceremony. "To be my lawfully wedded wife (so very briefly)." "To have and to hold (never again)." "'Til death do us part (My God, I think they mean it)." As soon as the parson closed his Bible, Don turned to her father and mumbled, "I'm sorry about this." Her brothers stood, arms folded, shoulder to shoulder, like a wall of granite. Her mother's sobs could be heard from the adjoining room. Don stumbled over the welcome mat as he left.

His family members in Nebraska became aware of it, of course. The father called a family gathering when Don came home early in disgrace. His parents and his five brothers and sisters were all there—the two youngest barely comprehending, the older ones smirking, their mother weeping, their father stern.

"What has happened is over and done with." His dad drew himself up to his full five feet five inches. "I don't want to hear any more talk about it in this house." He spoke as the patriarch. "I don't want any of you rubbing it in. No more talk. It's like cow manure. The more you stir it, the more it stinks." His voice rose threateningly. "And don't let me hear of any one of the rest of you getting into this kind of mess. Keep it in your pants." It was as if a judge had slammed down a final gavel.

In late March, surrounded by her family, Bernice brought forth her first born son, wrapped him in a baby blanket, and she called his name Donald Eugene McBride. She could not, for all her trying, remember his father's face, but she gave her baby his name. In April, the divorce was final. On the decree, under the question "What is the reason for the divorce?" the judge wrote: "The father is a wanderer."

Bernice and her baby boy were lost to the family, so that, after awhile, Don gave neither of them a thought. It was a summer fling gone bad. He conveniently closed that chapter of his life and spoke of it no more, nor did his family. In his heart, though, he knew he was going to hell. He had heard his Methodist pastor preach about falling from grace. Don had heard that sermon more than once: "If you miss the train by one minute, you've missed the train. If you miss salvation by one sin, you have missed salvation." Don was relieved to join the Baptists who preached once saved, always saved.

Maryland–1985

My brother was grilling by the pool. Some of our McBride relatives were visiting, and I had driven up from Richmond for the day. Carolyn was in Europe, so she missed this cook-out. Aunt Betty was there from Virginia Beach, and Uncle Milford, the youngest of the boys in the family of daddy's generation, had come in from Nebraska. Don, the convivial host, had bought a bottle of Canadian whiskey for Milford. During the course of the day, Milford drank most of it.

"Do you know what the worst thing in the world is?" Milford directed the question at me. His words were slurred. He had a naughty grin on his face.

"No, what is the worst thing in the world?"

"A hypocrite. That's what."

"Well, Milford, you know, you could be right." It was my standard, noncommital answer. I helped myself to potato salad and baked beans.

"Your daddy was a hypocrite."

"He was? My dad was a hypocrite?" My uncle was deep into his cups.

"Yes, he was." Milford wagged his finger in my direction. "Did you know he fathered a child out of wedlock?" I put my plate down and looked at my uncle, suddenly very interested.

"No, I don't think I've ever heard that story." I called to my brother, "Don, come over here. Have you ever heard this story? Milford, tell Don what you just told me."

"I said, your daddy was a hypocrite. Did you know he fathered a child out of wedlock?"

Don and I looked at each other in disbelief, mouths literally agape. "Have you ever heard anything about this?"

"No." We burst into laughter simultaneously. "Oh my gosh, we know something Carolyn doesn't know."

"A child out of wedlock. Well, that explains a lot." Don shook his head. "That may be why dad was always so hard on me. My gosh, we have a half-brother out there somewhere."

"Betty, did you know our father fathered a child out of wedlock?" I couldn't get over it.

"Of course. Everyone in the family knew that. How do you know it?"

"Milford just told us."

"Well, blabbermouth! That was supposed to be a family

secret."

I had read somewhere that families are as sick as their secrets. I thought, "If that's true, this family must be in extremis."

CARNEGIE–1993

We sat in May's living room. It was dim and cool. "I will never forget your mother. She was Brother Mac's second daughter, the sweet-natured one. Her mother, that was your Grandmother McGregor, always said that Keith was all joy. Oh, it broke our hearts when she died. She was so young, so beautiful. I thought your grandmother was going to have a breakdown over her death. Oh, honey, it was a sad time."

CARNEGIE–1935

The headline in *The Carnegie Herald* confirmed what he already knew was true, but didn't want to accept: "FUNERAL RITES FOR MRS. MCBRIDE HELD SUNDAY AFTERNOON." R.K. picked up the paper and read the article again:

"Losing a courageous, up-hill struggle that had passed from one desperate crisis to another during the past two months, Mrs. Don McBride passed away at the Patterson hospital Friday morning. Funeral services were conducted from the First Baptist Church at 2:30 Sunday afternoon by Rev. Garland C. Howard, pastor, and interment was made in the Carnegie cemetery under direction of the Pitcher Funeral Home. She had lived here for the past ten years. Keith McGregor was born at Cleburne, Texas, September 15, 1906.

In 1916 her parents moved to Chickasha where she graduated from high school and where she was a student at the Oklahoma College for Women for two years. The family moved to Carnegie in 1915. . ."

R.K. thought aloud, "They have that date wrong. It was 1925. That's a typographical error." He picked the article again:

". . . when her father, Rev. R. K. McGregor, became pastor of the First Baptist Church, and where she has since made her home. She was married to Don O. McBride November 24, 1927, and to this union three children were born: Donald Keith, aged five; Carolyn, aged two, and Roberta Sue, aged two months. Besides her husband and children, she is survived by her parents, Rev. and Mrs. McGregor, and two sisters, Mrs. Joe Briscoe and Mrs. Gordon Saunders. She has been a member of the Baptist church since childhood."

R.K. read the long list of the names of those who had attended the funeral. Great tears rolled unchecked down his cheeks. "Oh, God. This hurts more than anything I've ever had to bear. Lord, help me, and please take care of my girl in heaven. We'll help to take care of her children down here." He allowed himself to cry for a moment. Then he drew his handkerchief from his pocket, mopped his face, blew his nose mightily, and squared his shoulders. He had to pull himself together and go make hospital calls. His people needed him. And they expected him to be strong.

෫ා

The baby was asleep. May spread out the length of white batiste on the kitchen table. She laid out the tiny pattern and pinned it carefully to the delicate fabric. Then she began to cut. Every lady needs a new dress for Easter Sunday. Smiling at the thought as she read the instructions one more time, she carried the little dress and bonnet-to-be, still pinned to the pattern pieces, to her Singer sewing machine. She was proud of that machine and had already made herself a dress, Melford a night shirt, and Charles a pair of pajamas. This project was going to be a bit more difficult because it was so small. She would have to do some hand stitching on both the dress and the bonnet. Humming as she worked, she was a woman content with her world. May loved her husband; she loved her boy; and now, at last, she had a beautiful baby girl sleeping in the next room.

May loaded the machine with a spool of Coate's white. She pulled the thread through the spindle from right to left, then down through the inverted needle, slipped the filled bobbin into its slot with a click, and pulled both threads out and back. She picked up the front piece of the tiny dress and, pumping the treadle with her feet, she guided the fabric under the presser foot and sewed in the darts. "This is going to be so sweet," she thought. By the time the baby woke from her nap the main pieces of the dress were put together. Tonight she'd do the hand work on the dress, and tomorrow she'd work on the bonnet.

She heard a sleepy cry from the bedroom and hurried in to attend to the baby. "Well, did my sweet girl have a nap?" She smiled and crooned. "You are a wet baby child. Mama is just going to change your diaper, and you will be all better." While May changed the diaper, she conversed with the baby. "Did you know you are going to have a new dress for Easter Sunday? Yes, you are. You'll go to church and look so pretty. All the people will look at you and say, 'My, oh my, what a pretty girl.'" May lifted the little one from the crib and snuggled her against her shoulder. She put the baby on the sofa and lay a pillow beside her to keep her from rolling off. Then, she dragged the crib into the doorway which led from the kitchen into the bedroom. Placing the baby back in the crib, she continued her conversation. "Now you just stay right there while Mama fixes dinner for Daddy and Charles. Yes, ma'am, we are going to have meatloaf for dinner, and won't that be good?" May busied herself among the pots and pans.

May was thirty-two years old. She had hoped to fill the house with children, but after Charles, the doctor had been stern as he warned her not to have another baby. She had cried many a tear over that. She did so want babies–lots of them. May was the personification of "the great earth mother." She had so much love to give. She poured it out on Charles, but Charles was sixteen now. He was a good boy, and she was so proud of him. She taught children at church. Generations of children had passed through her Sunday School room and every one of them had been the recipients of her love. May had a hunger for children that her own boy alone could not completely satisfy. She looked at the babies, and her heart would yearn to hold them. And now, here was this baby girl. "God works in mysterious ways his wonders to perform," she thought, as she poured warm milk into the baby bottle, pulled the rubber nipple down hard over the top until it snapped over the lip of the bottle. As she carried the bottle to the child, she said, "Here is your bottle. Say 'Thank you,' say 'Thank you.'" May picked up the tiny girl and carried her to the rocking chair. She settled herself, with the baby safe in the curve of her arm. The baby sucked the milk from the nipple. The warm life-giving fluid filled the tiny belly. The warmth of life-giving love filled May's heart. They were both content.

CARNEGIE–1993

We sat in May's living room.

"Oh, honey. We pulled the crib right up next to our bed, and if you cried in the night, why, I would just put my hand over on you and you would get quiet and go back to sleep." Melford said to me, he said, 'Don't let her cry, May. She has already cried enough.' That's what he said. They had you in a room away from your mother, so she couldn't hear you cry. You know, it was just a "jake-leg" hospital. The doctors and nurses would go home at night and leave the patients there. When Melford was the night watchman in town, he'd go by the hospital and hear you crying all alone in there, and it made him sad to hear you. He didn't think it was right to leave a baby alone like that."

CARNEGIE–1935

May changed the baby's diaper and slipped her into the new dress. She brushed the wispy hair and put the bonnet on her and tied the silk ribbons under her chin. The ruffles on the bonnet framed the tiny face. She looked like a little doll. May picked the baby up and carried her in to show her off to Melford and Charles. "Here she is. How do you like the Easter girl?"

"Oh, my. Look at our girl." Melford's big square hands reached for her. "Aren't you just the prettiest thing?"

"Could I carry her?" Charles was built like his daddy and would be solid once he filled out. Right now he was slim and gangling.

"Not on your life," his daddy grinned. "I'm going to carry

31

her."

May shook her head. "I've never seen the like the way you two fuss over this girl. I'm going to settle this right now. I'm going to carry her." May took the baby and wrapped her in a blanket against the Oklahoma wind. And off to church they went.

As May was climbing the steps to the front of the church, she saw Don and his other two children coming toward the building. The little ones were dressed for Easter. His aunt Jenny Spence from Nebraska was there to help out. She had probably seen to it that the children had Easter clothes. No one knew how long she would stay. After all, she had a family of her own back home. How long could she stay away? Don was going to have a hard time with those two children. What can a man do? He has to work. He had two choices: either an orphanage or get some woman to come in and help.

May carried the baby through the hallway and looked for Don. He had taken Donald and Carolyn to their Sunday School room. Now she saw him as he walked toward her. She stopped him in the hall.

"Don, do you want to see the baby? I made her a dress for Easter." She pushed the blanket away from the little face. He looked stricken.

"Oh, Mrs. Anderson," he said. "I forgot about her."

"That's all right. I made her dress. Men shouldn't have to worry about things like that. Don't you worry. We'll take care of this baby."

*C*ARNEGIE–1993

*M*ay was sitting in her rocking chair. "Your daddy was going to let us adopt you. Poor man. He would come to the house to see you, and you were afraid of him. He would cry. It just about broke my heart. But what could he do? He had two other children to see to. He would say to Melford, "What am I going to do about this baby?" And Melford would always say, "We'll take care of her. I can feed her and put clothes on her and we'll see to it that she goes to school. We'll send her to OBU when she's ready to go to college. We can do it. You don't have to worry one bit about her."

Carnegie–1927

Effie had a headache. "I just don't think I can stand all those people coming in here tomorrow. I just don't think my nerves will hold up to it." R.K. glanced at his wife.

"Now Effie. You'll do just fine. The girls can help you today. I'll be back here after I make that hospital call, and I'll help. It's only a wedding and I've done many a wedding."

"Yes, but you don't have to bake the wedding cake."

R.K. slipped into his coat. As he walked through the front room, he spoke to his daughters. "Now, you all help your mother today. I ought to be back here in about an hour and we'll get this house cleaned up."

Keith hugged her father. "How's the bride?" He asked her.

"I'm just fine, Daddy."

"You're sure about this?"

"I'm very sure. I do love him, and I know he loves me."

"All right, then. He just better be good to you."

"He will, Daddy." It never dawned on Keith that Don had been married before and was the father of a child almost five. And it never entered his mind to tell her. Better to let sleeping dogs lie. Don was moving on. He had an incredible ability to compartmentalize, but neither Keith nor her parents knew this as the wedding plans went forward.

R.K. stepped out into the cold November morning. "Who ever heard of a wedding this time of year?" he murmured. "Don seems a nice enough kid. I hope he knows what a treasure he's getting. My sweet Keith. She is my jewel and my joy. She is beautiful and smart–must have taken after her daddy." He grinned at this, but believed it to be true, nevertheless.

The Carnegie Herald, dated November 30, 1927, ran the following story on the same page with an article headlined "ALLEGED CHICKEN THIEF HELD FOR DISTRICT COURT:"

"McBRIDE-McGREGOR"

"A wedding of much interest to friends here was solemnized at 10 a. m., Thursday, Nov. 24, when Miss Keith McGregor, daughter of Rev. and Mrs. R.K. McGregor, became the bride of Don Olin [sic] McBride. The ceremony was performed at the home of the bride and her father officiated. After the ceremony, the young people accompanied by Mr. And Mrs. Jas. McBride of Cowles, Neb., the groom's parents, left for Oklahoma City for a short trip.

"Miss Keith is a graduate of the Chickasha high school and a former student at the Oklahoma College for Women. She has made a wide circle of friends since coming here two years ago. For the past year she has been employed at the Ford agency as bookkeeper.

"Mr. McBride is an ambitious young man who has just recently located permanently in Carnegie. He is one of the proprietors of the Carnegie laundry. He was formerly connected with the S. W. L. & Power Co., as civil engineer. Mr. And Mrs. McBride returned here Saturday night where they are receiving the felicitations of their friends.

"The guests who were present at the wedding beside the immediate families of the bride and groom were Mrs. J.D. Beggs, Oklahoma City; Mr. and Mrs. B. E. Coughman, Electra, Texas; Rev. and Mrs. Sam D. Taylor, Anadarko, and Mrs. J. A. Wright, Everett Wright and Miss Louise Vaughan."

It had been a sweet little wedding. The parsonage was shining clean thanks to the combined efforts of the bride and her sisters. Guests gathered in the living room, anticipating the party to follow. The table was laid with damask and silver. The wedding cake rested in the center of the table surrounded by fall flowers. Trays of finger sandwiches and cookies were prepared the day before and covered all the counter space in the kitchen.

R.K. stood in front of the fireplace. He had on his Sunday suit and held his Bible. Keith's sisters served as bridesmaids wearing identical orange chiffon dresses with brown sashes. They carried nosegays of bronze chrysanthemum and stood smiling as Keith made her appearance from the bedroom. She was radiant in her mother's wedding gown, the first of the three daughters to wear it. She stood confidently in the presence of God and twenty wedding guests and promised to love, honor, and obey her husband all the days of her life.

After the party, Don and Keith got into the back seat of his father's car. Keith's new in-laws sat in front, Don's dad at the wheel. That afternoon, they made their wedding trip, all the way to the Huckins Hotel in downtown Oklahoma City. They spent one night in room 727. The room charge was $4.50. They made two phone calls, one for a dime, and one for twenty cents. Their total honeymoon bill came to $4.80. Keith asked Don for the receipt so she could paste it in her album. The next day Don's parents drove them back to Carnegie where, as *The Carnegie Herald* reported, they received the felicitations of their friends.

$\mathcal{N}$EBRASKA–1930

$\mathcal{W}$hen Donald Keith was fourteen months old, Don and Keith packed up the Ford and drove from Carnegie to Benkleman for Christmas. It was not an easy trip, but they really wanted to spend Christmas with Don's family. Everyone was there. Don's brother, Shep, and his wife, Isabel, lived there, of course. Their little boy, Jimmy, was four and their baby girl, Patricia—Patty—was a bit older than Donald Keith. They also had a new baby boy, Bobby. Don's other brother, Buns, and his wife, Helen, were there with their baby girl, Jane, three months old. The three oldest boys were all married and had started their families. This would be the first time they had all been together for years, and the last time for some years to come.

It was uncontrolled mayhem. When one baby cried, the others all joined in. The three young mothers, the daughters-in-law, were constantly running from bedroom to kitchen, warming bottles, changing diapers, burping babies. Grandmother McBride had her hands full cooking huge meals and seeing to it that everyone had a place to sleep and plenty to eat. On Christmas Day, after all the presents had been opened and the mess cleaned up, they sat down to turkey dinner and stuffed themselves with holiday goodies. Then, they all went out to the side yard to have their picture taken.

That photograph shows all the McBrides lined up and looking straight into the camera. Granddad and Grandmother McBride were in their early fifties. They had three unmarried children and three married sons. At that time, there were five grandchildren. Don and Keith are in the center of that picture, dressed in their Sunday best. Donald Keith is in his daddy's arms. Keith appears confident and looks just like Amelia Earhart. Five years later, she would be dead.

OKLAHOMA CITY–1939

Mama was ironing, so it must have been a Tuesday. I was sitting in the front room, rocking myself back and forth, bouncing against the back of the couch allowing the momentum to push me forward. It was something I often did. I also rocked myself to sleep in my bed at night. The self propelled motion was comforting. Suddenly, I stopped rocking.

"Mama, were we both Pattersons before we married daddy?"

She smiled, unplugged the iron, and came to sit by me on the couch.

"You know, when you were a little baby, I gave you your very first bath in the hospital."

"Uh-huh." I had heard that story before.

"Most little babies went home soon after they were born, but you stayed in the hospital. Did you know that?"

"How long did I stay?"

"Oh, you stayed for six months, and all the nurses wanted to have nursery duty so they could hold you and play with you. We all loved you very much."

She looked at me to see if I was understanding.

"You know that most mommies carry their babies in their tummies before the babies are born. You know that I didn't carry you in my tummy. Another lady carried you in her tummy. But then, I got to be your mommie when I married your daddy. Is that okay with you?"

"Oh, that's okay, Mama. I didn't know that other lady anyway." I hopped down off the couch and went to find my dolls.

CARNEGIE—1929

When her labor pains began, Don took Keith to the parsonage. He hated seeing her like this. He hated to look at her bloated body. Keith was a small woman, fine-boned and slightly built. Standing just over five feet, she looked like a child herself, carrying this child high and forward as though struggling with an oversized watermelon. She retained fluid throughout the months of waiting. Formerly beautiful, slender ankles were stumps, and her face took on the shape of the full moon. Her small breasts had become grotesquely engorged and were constantly leaking fluid. They were tender to the touch. In the last weeks, she could not find a comfortable position, standing, sitting, or reclining. She did not know her own body. She did not want anyone, not even Don, to see her like this. Especially not Don. Most of all, she just wanted this to be over. She felt that she had been pregnant forever. It would be over, but not soon.

The front bedroom of the parsonage had been scrubbed clean and emptied of everything but a bed and a table and a chair. R.K. and Effie stacked clean towels and fresh bed linens on the table.

"I know this is the way everybody came into the world, but when it is your own child having a child, it's like the first baby ever born." Effie was nervous. "I just hope the Lord is good to her and she has an easy time."

"I'll be glad when it's over. It's hard to think, Effie, that we are going to be grandpa and grandma. You are too good-looking to be a grandmother."

"You always were a sweet talker. I am not going to be grandma. I'm going to be 'Nana.' I have chosen my own name so I don't get called 'Moomaw' or some other awful thing."

They heard Don and Keith at the front door. Effie ran to open it.

"Oh, come in children." She took one look at Keith. "Oh, my dear, you are in distress already. Let's get you into bed."

With R.K., Effie, and Don all three trying to be of help, they got Keith into the improvised birthing chamber. Effie took over. "Don, go into the kitchen and make coffee. R.K., you go get the doctor. I want him here and in charge." When the men left to complete their assigned chores, Effie put her hands on Keith's belly and prayed. "Lord, may this child be born healthy, and may you in your great mercy spare this mother." She got Keith out of her clothes and into a gown. All was in readiness. This was not a dress rehearsal.

The curtain is rung. The eternal drama is played out once more and forever. It began with Eve. It reaches forward in time to all her daughters. The protagonist is a woman. Supporting roles are assumed by midwives, doctors, and nurses. The father-to-be is an offstage character, having made his contribution at the time of the prologue. Walk-on roles are assigned to the parents of the mother, neighbor women, and church ladies bearing casseroles. Pain never leaves the stage. Death lurks in the wings, waiting for his cue. The props have changed over time, but the dialogue is standard. The agonized masked face of tragedy turns into the grin of comedy only at the final curtain. And it comes after cataclysm and peril.

It was over, thank God. Don, relieved, kissed an exhausted Keith, held his new child, and went down to the telegraph office to send a telegram to his parents in Nebraska: "It's a boy. Ten pounds. Donald Keith. Mother, baby fine." The telegraph operator looked at him and smiled. "Congratulations on your new son."

Don nodded. "Thanks."

"And how is your wife?"

"She's fine. Easy as pie. It was like shelling peas."

The birth announcement appeared three days later, October 16, 1929, in *The Carnegie Herald:*

"The stork was busy in this community the first of the week. Donald Keith, a 10-pound son was born to Mr. and Mrs. Don McBride Sunday. Hoot, th' bonnie wee laddie be Scotch."

The publisher of the newspaper was Don's good friend, Harry Jolly. As the family grew, Don spent many a night having a night cap with Harry. He left Keith to cope with domestic matters.

RICHMOND–1992

*D*on?" I asked. "This is your sister—the pretty one."

He laughed. "How are you doing, you sweet thing?"

"I'm doing good, and I'm doing well." It was an old joke. "How about yourself?"

"Great. Are you all ready for Christmas?"

"As ready as I'm going to get. Don, can you get away in January to go to Oklahoma? I haven't seen Ann in a good long while. I thought I'd call Carolyn and see if we three can get together out there at Ann's. She was good to us when we were kids and she's not getting any younger."

"That's right. That's a good idea. When in January are you thinking of going?"

"It depends on when we can get tickets. I was thinking maybe we could go in the middle of the month. I've got my calendar in front of me. If we left early on the fourteenth, we could spend a long weekend. I'd have to get back here Sunday night."

"Okay. Call Carolyn, and I'll see what I can do on this end."

The phone rang three times in Bonita Bay before my sister picked it up.

"Carolyn, it's Bert. What are you up to?"

"Oh, you wouldn't believe what's going on around here. It's an absolute frenzy."

Before she could get into the details of the latest crisis in her family—and there always was a crisis—I asked if she could meet us in Oklahoma and gave her the dates.

"Okay. That sounds good. You need to know that I'm going back to my doctor in Indiana to have foot surgery."

"Don't they have doctors in Florida?"

"Yes, but I don't know them. I've got a bunion. I'll tell you all about it when I see you."

So we were going to Oklahoma–back to the land of our birth. We were going back to the land of all the old animosities, the old pain, the old jealousies–back to the land my brother ran away from at sixteen. We were going back to our roots. I knew there would be the inevitable "Mother always did love you best" talk. But we were adults, now, and since our parents' deaths we had vowed to be closer. And Ann had been good to all of us when we were children. Once, Donald had an accident on his bike. Because he had cut his leg and torn his pants, he was afraid to go home and tell the folks. He knew their reaction would be anger over the torn pants. So, he went to Ann's and she cleaned up the blood, attended to the cut, and then she sewed up the rip in his pants. After that, she called our house and explained what had happened. She was a good egg—more like an older sister than an aunt. I remember when, before she was married, she lived in an apartment near our elementary school. Carolyn and I would go over there after school sometimes. Once, we walked into her unlocked apartment when she wasn't home and found two Easter dolls—one dressed in pink and the other in white. When we told her we had found them, she assured us they were for two other little girls, but we knew they were for us.

$\mathcal{O}$KLAHOMA–1993

$\mathcal{W}$e rendezvoused in the Dallas-Fort Worth airport. Carolyn came in from Fort Myers, Don from BWI and I, from Richmond, by way of Atlanta. We met with smiles and hugs. Don said, "I'm going to check to see if our flight is on time," and left to read the monitor. He was soon back with our flight information. We took our time getting to the gate from which our flight to Oklahoma City would depart. Carolyn was having difficulty walking.

"I'm going to Indiana from here to see my doctor on Monday. I don't know what's wrong with me. I'm running low on energy or something."

"That will be the day. I've never seen anyone with more energy than you," I teased. I was sure this was just the latest crisis—another event blown out of proportion. Never had I known anyone more histrionic than my sister.

"You get that damn bunion taken care of and you'll be good as new." Don reached for the Hertz reservation in his wallet. "Carolyn, I have arranged for a rental car."

"Oh, no. I'm renting the car. I've got us a Lincoln Continental like mine. I won't drive another car. It's too confusing."

"Is it blue?" he asked. It was her favorite color.

"Well, I requested blue, but we'll see what they give us."

It was brown. "I hate brown. I've been Carolyn Brown ever since I married and I hate the name and I hate the color." Carolyn stood at the rental car counter at Will Rogers International Airport. "Don't you have a blue one?"

"I'm sorry, ma'am. That's all we have in the car you requested." The girl at the counter gave Carolyn a strange look. She seemed somewhat baffled. "I don't believe anyone has ever requested a car by color before. Let me look one more time." She checked her computer. "No, I'm sorry. This seems to be the only Lincoln we have."

My brother spoke up. "We'll take it." That settled it. We pulled our luggage carts through the revolving door leading to the underground parking area. We found the brown Lincoln and loaded our luggage into its ample trunk. Carolyn took the wheel, and we headed north on I-40, then I-35 to Edmond, Oklahoma.

"I tend to forget how flat this place is," I said as I settled into the luxury of the back seat.

"And everything's so brown."

"It's January. Of course it's brown."

I tapped my brother's shoulder. "Don, do you have your camera? I'd like to take a swing through the old neighborhood."

"Yeah, I brought it. Why don't we take one day while we're here and just make the rounds."

In Oklahoma City, we swung onto the Broadway Extension after we had driven past Nichols Hills where daddy always took us to see the Christmas lights when we were young. "I remember coming to Edmond with Sam and Ann when I was a kid. It was open country from Oklahoma City up to Edmond. It's all grown up, now."

"That's right. But that was way before the city incorporated all this territory. Did you know that Oklahoma City is the largest city in the United States?"

"I think that's right—geographically. Obviously, not in population."

"You know what I'd like to do while we're here?" Don said. "I'd like to go to Carnegie and look around and see if I remember anything. I left there when I was six. Of course, I went back as a teenager to live with Ray and Jewel one summer."

"Sure, we could do that. Ann might want to go if she's feeling okay." Carolyn slowed as we turned onto Fifteenth Street in Edmond.

"We're almost to Rankin. It's just up at the next light if I remember correctly, and we take a left."

"Right. No, no. I mean, correct, you do turn left." We were only a block away from Ann's and our great adventure.

Ann had always been a fabulous cook. We sat down around the old oak pedestal table. It was loaded with everything good: roast beef, potatoes and gravy, fresh green beans, fried okra, squash casserole, home made relishes, hot rolls and blackberry cobbler topped with vanilla ice cream for dessert.

"Ann, you have outdone yourself. This is great food. You shouldn't have gone to all this trouble."

"Oh, poo. I cook for myself. I just hope you don't mind eating what I eat."

"I haven't eaten like this since I was a kid." My brother

reached for another roll. "This is wonderful."

"If I ate like this all the time I'd weigh a ton. Maybe it would be worth it." I hadn't enjoyed food this much since I was eating Mama's cooking.

"Let's plan what we are going to do while we are here," Carolyn suggested.

"Yeah, Ann. Don wants to go to Carnegie to look around, and I want to be sure to get some pictures of the houses we lived in when we were kids, maybe go by Trinity."

"We need to swing by our elementary school and Harding Junior High. Is it still there?"

Ann nodded. "As far as I know, they still hold school there."

"What do you say we take our tour of Oklahoma City tomorrow and then on Saturday we can head down to Carnegie. Carolyn, make a list of all the places we want to see so we're sure we don't miss anything."

"Be glad to," she said and started rummaging in her purse for pen and notepad.

Ann put away the leftovers while I loaded the dishwasher. Don and Carolyn sat in the den thinking through the places we wanted to revisit. Don loaded his camera. When the last crumb was swept and the kitchen was clean, I announced, "I don't know about you all, but I'm going in and put on my gown."

"We will, too, in a minute as soon as I get this list down."

I took my flannel granny gown from my suitcase, washed the top layer of travel grime from my face, got out my fuzzy slippers, and brushed my hair. One of the things I loved most about the winter months was my flannel gown and fuzzy slippers. When I was ready for bed, I stepped back into the den.

"Oh, hey. You look so comfortable, I'm going to do the

same," Carolyn said.

"Me too, Carolyn." Ann went back to her room and Carolyn to the front bedroom we were to share. I went to the kitchen, poured a cup of decaf, came back, and settled into a chair.

"Say cheese." I looked up and Don snapped a picture. "This is the first snapshot of our trip."

"I love this house. I guess I'm as much at home here as I am anywhere."

"Yeah, I know. There are some things that never change."

Ann's house was the one she and Sam had shared for all those years until his death. It was the house where they had raised their kids. Not large, it was a simply-built, three bedroom, red brick rancher. Memories filled it—the bronze statue of the naked lady holding the ashtray beside the easy chair in the living room, the deep purple twin armchairs, the paintings by friends and family, the heavy TV set in the dark cabinet that surely must have been one of the first made, the sofas and chairs made for comfort. There were photographs of children and grandchildren interspersed among books and bric-a-brac on the built-in shelves beside the fireplace. The old clock chimed eight. This house was cluttered with mementoes of a life-time. Ann's taste ran to the expensive. Put away on shelves in the dining area was Heisy and Haviland and Gorham—a service for twelve, and enough cut glass for a queen's dinner party.

Ann and Carolyn came back into the den in their gowns and robes and settled into a comfortable evening of desultory talk. Ann, her feet propped up on the footstool, began. We were like kids around a campfire passing the torch of memory. We did not name it, but this was ritual, as formalized, in its way, as any worship.

"Do you remember the time Sam and I took you kids fishing out to Lake Hiwassee? Carolyn was in the boat and Donald pushed the boat out? He did it just to hear you scream."

"I remember it," Carolyn remarked. "You were an ornery kid, you know."

"Well, yes, but if you remember correctly, I went in after you and I was fully clothed."

"Yeah, you were fully clothed and sopping wet and Ann wouldn't let you in the car like that. Do you remember what you wore on the trip back home?"

"I remember it was a skirt."

"It was the skirt to my playsuit. And you put a scarf on your head." The laughter was right on cue. This was an oft-repeated story, a part of family lore. It didn't really matter how seldom or how often we were together. This was one of the stories that made up the story of our lives. As we talked, we were young again. We could see the colors, hear the sounds, and feel the emotions of that lost time. Of the million events that make up our lives, why do we remember this?

"I wonder how that affected me? The very idea of making a twelve-year-old boy wear a girl's skirt!"

"I wish that had been the worst thing that ever happened to you."

$\mathcal{O}$KLAHOMA CITY–1944

$\mathcal{D}$addy drove his Ford into our driveway. Our parents had gone to church for the watch night service. It was their custom to be in prayer as the new year came in. Carolyn and I stayed home. Donald had run away again. This time, he had been gone for three days. We woke up to the familiar sounds of violence. This time the sounds came from our driveway. I heard daddy yelling, and then, I realized he was yelling at Donald. I heard the rage in his voice. "Where have you been?"

"What do you care?"

"You will answer me. I am your father."

"You sure as hell don't act like it."

"Don't you curse me." And then the blows. We knew daddy had taken off his belt. The buckle cut flesh. We heard Donald cry as much from humiliation as from pain.

Carolyn began to hyperventilate. I wanted to make daddy stop. I felt small and weak. My brother had sometimes stood in front of me to protect me from such blows, his eyes challenging, his back unbent. My brother was brave. My brother was a hero. Why couldn't I do something to make daddy stop? I closed my eyes tight and put my head under my pillow and tried not to be sick.

$\mathcal{E}$DMOND–1993

$\mathcal{I}$, bygod, remember digging dandelions. Dad didn't think it was work unless you sweated in the hot sun. I used a butcher knife with a broken blade to dig with. Lord, I hated that job." Don shook his head.

"I remember when daddy would come in to wake us up in the morning and would turn the light on and off really fast and yell, 'Hit the deck, pee cats!' What a rude awakening." The memory made me shudder.

"Nothing like starting the day with an insult," Carolyn remarked.

"Yes, we were all bed wetters. Mother made us wash our

sheets in the bathtub every morning and hang them on the line to dry before we went to school, even when it was cold outside and the sheets froze on the line." I remembered the humiliation and the cold.

Ann was uncomfortable with that kind of talk. "You better be grateful to her. You all would have been in an orphanage if she hadn't married your father."

"An orphanage might have been an improvement." Carolyn had a tart tongue.

"You know," Don said, "I forgave our parents long ago. I loved them in spite of everything."

Ann kicked off her house shoes. "I remember saying to your dad once, 'Don,' I said, 'You are a good guy and I like everything about you, but one there's one thing I don't like about you, and that's how you beat your kids.' 'Ann,' he said to me, 'I know I shouldn't beat my kids. I always feel bad about it after I do it. I feel real bad.'"

"But not bad enough to stop it." I said it aloud. "I was terrified of daddy, but I loved him, too. It's called ambivalence, children." I stood to take my empty cup back into the kitchen. "Mama was always good to me."

Carolyn looked up as I walked by her. "Well, of course she was good to you. She was partial to you. Mother always did love you best." I rolled my eyes heavenward. "Oh Lord," I thought. "Here we go."

"That's why I've never been partial to my kids. I know how much harm it can do." Carolyn had an unlimited capacity for self delusion. She was convinced she was not partial to any one of her four children. I looked at Donald, my eyebrows upraised, and he smiled. Carolyn had three boys before her only daughter was born. Donna, named after our father, was the long-awaited child. She received preferential treatment from the moment she was born. She was the child who had elaborate birthday parties while the boys had none. It was clear to Carolyn's third son that he was just another boy—a reject—until her girl was born. Carolyn did the same with her grandchildren—first, Jennifer was the child of promise, and then Rachel. She tolerated the boys and adored the girls—until they grew old enough to be mouthy.

I had a long-held theory that Carolyn loved little girls because she was attempting, through them, to rectify her own painful childhood. In loving her daughter and her grand-daughters, she was really loving the little girl who was herself. She had a very expensive collection of handmade dolls. Most of them were blonde and blue-eyed, and dressed in baby blue—organdy, silk, batiste, taffeta. They were off limits to the grandchildren, of course. "These are Gramma's dolls. You may not touch these." They stood on display shelves behind glass doors, beautiful and inaccessible. They, too, served to delight and nurture Carolyn, the little girl who was so abandoned, rejected, and mistreated.

Carolyn was a spender. She had unlimited credit on her credit cards, but she preferred to pay cash. She carried so much money around with her that I feared someone would knock her over the head and steal her purse.

"Carolyn," I gasped. "How much money do you have in that purse? Don't let anyone see it. Someone is going to hurt you and steal it."

She looked at me and said, "I know it's crazy, but I feel insecure when I have less than five hundred dollars in my purse. I don't like to use a credit card. It makes me nervous. When they have to check to see if the card is valid, it makes me feel like they think I don't have the money. The only thing that gives me any security is cash, and I have plenty of it."

Fortunately, she had married a man who had a talent for making money. She would count the number of pairs of shoes in her closet and report to me, and, I was sure, to others. "I have forty-five pairs of shoes." Her closets were full of expensive clothes, some with the tags never removed. She was a perfect size twelve. She lived in a hurry, and never took the time to try on anything. She knew what would fit her and what would not. She would see something on the rack, grab it, pay for it, and take it home. It might stay in her closet for months, or she might put it on immediately and wear it out to dinner that night. She had a beautiful figure—slim hips and legs, long waist, square shoulders. She looked great in her clothes. If she had been taller, she could have been a model.

Carolyn was prone to anxiety attacks. Given to outbursts of rage, she dramatized and overdid everything she touched. She volunteered on a big scale. Once when she was newly married, she called Ann.

"How do you make an apple pie?"

"Wait a minute, and I'll find my recipe. Are you planning to make one for dinner tonight?"

Carolyn replied. "No, I'm going to make twelve for a Sunday School class gathering tonight at our house."

Once, she volunteered to be responsible for the crafts for the whole vacation Bible school at her church. She went out and bought kits so all the older children could make wallets. She bought something age-appropriate for the younger children—all of them. She must have spent a fortune. It reminded me of daddy's expansiveness when in a crowd. In years when he didn't have the money to spend, he would always pick up the tab. It made him feel like a king—the last of the big spenders.

Carolyn tended toward the outrageous. Once, when her

only daughter was eleven, Carolyn gave her the Sears credit card and sent her to the mall alone to buy a washing machine and a dryer. Obediently, the child found the appliance department and picked out the machines she wanted. Of course, the clerk called Carolyn. "Mrs. Brown?"

Impatiently, "Yes?"

"There is a little girl here with your credit card, and she wants to buy a washing machine and dryer."

"That would be correct. She's my daughter. Now, if you'll just sell them to her, I am late for a meeting."

My crazy sister. She had every material thing in this world—diamonds, swimming pools, and Lincoln Continentals, trips to Europe, a huge house in Florida, a house in Palm Springs, another in Wilmington—and none of it touched the emptiness inside her. She never got over our mother's death. She had daddy's temper. Folks, including her husband and children, fell in and out of favor with her on a regular basis. Carolyn was the most passionate person I ever knew. She loved and hated like fire and ice. She adored our brother. He was her hero. And she loved daddy with a possessive love.

On Carolyn's sixteenth birthday, daddy gave her Keith's ring. R.K. and Effie had given it to our mother when she graduated from high school. In art deco, it had a silver filagree setting, two small rubies and several little diamonds. Carolyn treasured it above all else. I sometimes wondered what ever happened to Keith's wedding ring. We have almost nothing that belonged to her. When she died at twenty-eight, she had not had much time, and certainly no money, to accumulate things of value. There is so little to remember her by—her ring, a few small snapshots, several pieces of everyday silverware, and her cookbook. And we three children, of course. We are her legacy.

The Christmas I was six–three weeks from my seventh birthday (Carolyn was nine and Donald was eleven)–we spent our holiday in Nebraska at Uncle Shep's house. By that time, Mary Lou had been our mother for five years. Carolyn got a little toy oven for Christmas. It had a real light bulb in it and it was hot enough to bake tiny cookies. Uncle Shep helped her bake cookies for daddy. They put soap powder in them for a joke. Everyone thought it was funny. Daddy laughed and laughed. It was good to see him laugh. Ordinarily, daddy was extremely authoritarian with his children. Even on this trip, our cousins were awed by his harshness.

Mother said then, and often, afterwards, "Our children might misbehave, but they will only do it once." The implication was that children must be intimidated into good behavior. It worked with me, but never worked with Donald. The dictum frightened Carolyn, but she was tough enough to buck it. I admired her strength, but did not like her anger. In that respect, she was so like our father. Daddy and Carolyn looked alike when they were mad. I've seen their blue eyes turn purple in anger–anger that made them momentarily powerful. Both anger and the accompanying power surge are addictive–like being drunk on your own hormones. Eventually, it can have a negative impact on the cardiovascular system–collateral damage, you might say.

Once, when Carolyn was five, she asked daddy, "How many brothers do you have?"

Daddy responded, "I have three brothers."

"How many sisters do you have?"

"I have two sisters." Then he reached over and patted her on the knee. "And I only have one mother."

He must have known how hard it was for Carolyn to have a stepmother. It was a tender moment between daddy and my sister. She needed tenderness. Dad walked a thin line between wanting to show love to his older two children, and staying in Mary Lou's good graces. What a mess. Carolyn desperately needed for him to love her above all others, and she was in vicious competition with Mary Lou and with me. In fact, she was in competition with all other females for male attention. Carolyn may have been the only female misogynist I ever encountered. During her teen years, she avoided girl friends. They were the competition. In college, she roomed with Mary Catherine Jolliffe from Del Ray. They did become friends. Mary Catherine was not competition. They were not attracted to the same boys. Carolyn went through most of her life hating our stepmother. She told me once, "There is no way a daughter can compete with a father's wife. There is no way a mother can compete with her daughter-in-law. The woman who provides sex for a man is the one who gets all the love and attention from him."

Carolyn went through most of her life hating me. She planned her wedding two weeks after my departure for college. Mother pointed out to her that I would not be able to come back home for the event. Carolyn's response was, "Good. I don't want her at my wedding. I picked this date on purpose." So, I was in my first semester of college on Valentine's Day, 1952, in North Carolina when Carolyn and Bob were married at home. Years later, after she had four children, our first child was born. Bob was at mother and daddy's house for some reason, without the rest of the family.

Mother said to Bob, "You know Roberta had her baby. It's a little boy."

Bob responded, "I wouldn't mention that to Carolyn if I were you. She doesn't want to hear about it. She is sure that now, Roberta's baby will be center stage, and you and Don will not be interested in our kids anymore."

All she wanted was to be loved, and she felt that she never was—not exclusively, and never enough. It was as if there was not enough love to go around, and she knew she would never get her fair share.

Carolyn and I operated under an uneasy truce. We had found sisterhood in 1971 when Bill and I were on our first furlough from Brazil. Daddy had called Carolyn and told her we would be in Knoxville and gave her the dates. "Come on down while she's here." It was an invitation that must have sounded to her more like a command. Carolyn responded with more than a hint of hysteria in her voice.

"I will not come to Knoxville to see Roberta. When she and I are in the same room, I feel like a cockroach. If she wants to see me, she can come to Fort Wayne and I will meet her on my own turf."

Daddy was shocked. "I had no idea you felt that way."

"Well, now you know."

It was as if a little girl was saying, "Love me, Daddy. Love me, not her. Love me."

Before our arrival in Knoxville, daddy had already made arrangements for us to go to Carolyn's house. We drove to Fort Wayne and arrived early in the evening. In her house, beds were stripped. Mattresses were bare. Pillows were without pillow cases. That night, there was no bedtime for the children. Kids dropped from exhaustion and slept where they fell. Carolyn and I sat up all night talking. She poured out her many grievances. I had been favored. She had been cast aside. I had been encouraged. No one ever encouraged her. I got to go to my high school senior prom. Daddy didn't let her go to hers. I had gone to college. She had been told to take a secretarial course because she was going to get married and have babies anyway. She had a home wedding. I got married in church. I agreed with much of her assessment. We hashed and rehashed all the old inequities. I told her I had felt responsible for Keith's death since she had died as a result of my birth. Carolyn assured me that she did not hold me responsible for our mother's death. I asked her forgiveness for any pain I had caused her. It did not occur to her to ask my forgiveness. At dawn, she declared that for the first time in her life she felt she had a sister instead of a competitor. Burdens were lifted. Forgiveness sweetened the air. All was well at last. Until the next time.

There were times when all the old anger and animosity would surface—at Mary Lou's death, at daddy's death, certainly. But there were other times, too. At odd times, when I would least expect it, out of the blue, there would come a dig, a sarcastic comment, a put-down that showed me that under all her attempts at maintaining a relationship with me, the old resentment simmered.

"Yeah, I used to tell people I hadn't seen my sister in twenty years and I didn't care if I never saw her again. That's what I used to tell people. Of course, I don't say that anymore."

I wanted to point out that she just did say it again, but I forbore. All her animosity was not aimed at me. Sometimes she would confide in me.

"No one is going to give me any sympathy when Bob dies. I've told everyone I hate him and I'll be glad when he's dead." It was her standard litany. After awhile, there was no more shock value to it.

I often asked, "Carolyn, if you are so unhappy with Bob why don't you leave him?" "What? And let some chickie-babe come in and walk off with everything that I have worked so hard for all these years? Not on your life. I'm sticking, and if

Bob wants to leave, he can pay me big."

They were held in their marriage by money and mutual dislike.

$\mathcal{E}$DMOND–1993

$\mathcal{M}$id-morning, we piled into Carolyn's rented Lincoln and headed south toward downtown Oklahoma City. Ann had insisted on cooking a big breakfast of sausage and biscuit and gravy. We were fortified with a huge overdose of cholesterol and enough calories to last us a week.

Ann, at twenty-one, had come from Tennessee to live with us when her father married the widow Ferguson. She went to beauty school, and then got a job at Ray Porter's barber shop on Walker and Twenty-third Street. I remembered the red and white striped barber pole in front of that shop. It rotated endlessly and never seemed to arrive at any destination. Ann had lived the rest of her adult life in Oklahoma City. She was now eighty-two, and she had no difficulty recalling early events.

"The house we first lived in when your folks came to Oklahoma City is still standing. Do you remember the oil derricks around in that neighborhood? I guess Oklahoma is the only state that has an oil derrick on the state capitol grounds." Her voice was soft, reminiscing.

"Dad had a chance to buy property out there. He didn't have two dimes to rub together back then. If he had been able to swing that deal, we'd all be rich," I said.

Don grinned. "What I remember about that house is the time I sent Bertie into the street to retrieve my ball. I knew I wasn't supposed to play in the traffic."

"I have heard that story all my life, but I have no conscious memory of it. I must have been two and that would have made you five or six. That experience probably is what messed me up, but if you give me all your money, I'll forgive you."

"Twenty-third Street was also Highway 66. There was a lot of traffic going through there. Even back then." Carolyn drummed her fingers on the steering wheel and sang, "Come get your kicks on Route 66." She knew the lyrics to every popular song from the forties to the sixties.

"Swing over and take Classen. That's where that old man let us out that time Ethel and I went swimming." Ann pointed to the corner of Classen and Twenty-third. "It was a long walk back home."

That family story was one that always brought laughter. Ann had been a young thing when she came out to Oklahoma. When Granddaddy Patterson remarried, Ann had objected to her father's new wife and was set on causing the newlyweds as much aggravation as she could manage. She was something of a hellion. Granddaddy was relieved to have her gone. She certainly livened up our household. Her artist friend, Ethel Hefflin, came to live with us, too. They made a striking pair—Ann was a blue-eyed, fair-skinned blonde, and Ethel was as brunette as a Spaniard. One Sunday afternoon, the two of them decided to go to a public swimming pool all the way out past May Avenue. Daddy drove them out there and dropped them off. He told them he would pick them up at five-thirty sharp. Dad had responsibilities at church on Sunday evenings. He told them he wanted them dressed and on the curb waiting for him when he drove up. At five-thirty, daddy, always punctual, drove up to the gate of the public pool. The girls were still in the water, and when he honked, they waved and swam to the far side of the pool. Daddy didn't hesitate. He pulled out of his parking spot and drove straight back home without them.

They got out of the pool, dried, and dressed; then, they discovered that neither of them had a dime. They began a very long walk back to the seven hundred block of Twenty-fifth Street. About that time, an old man in a rattletrap car, pulled up beside them.

"Can I offer you lovely young ladies a ride?" He doffed his hat gallantly, thereby exposing his hairless dome. "John Knox Turnipseed at your service. Yessiree, my folks were Presbyterians."

They knew better than to accept, but they were tired of walking, and he looked fairly harmless. They piled into his antiquated vehicle with thanks. Ann made sure Ethel sat in the middle by the old guy. His hands were mottled with age, and he was practically toothless.

"Well, do you girls like the moving picture shows?" The old fellow spoke to Ethel. "I could come by and get you and take you to the moving picture show." He put his arm around her and pulled her closer to him.

Ethel thought fast. She leaned forward. "No, I don't like picture shows."

Ann dug her elbow into Ethel's side. "Oh, Ethel, you know you have been dying to see that picture at the Tower."

Ethel dug her elbow into Ann's ribs. "No. I don't want to see it."

He tried again. "Well, I could take you out to dine." He patted Ethel's knee.

Ethel turned her knees as far to the right as she could manage without dislocating a hip joint or pulling a muscle. "No, I can't eat food out. I have a bad stomach. The doctor told me never to eat in a restaurant." Ethel was looking for an exit.

Ann said, "Oh, Ethel, I think it would be wonderful for you to go out with this nice man. Your doctor wouldn't mind. You would have a lovely time."

They were approaching Classen Avenue. Ethel, desperate by this time, turned to their host. "You can let us out right here. We live right close by."

When the girls were safely on the sidewalk and their benefactor had driven away, Ann turned to Ethel. "Why did you make him let us out so far from home?"

Ethel said, "I didn't want him to know where we live." She didn't speak to Ann again for days. We told and retold that story through the years and laughed every time we told it.

We drove down Classen. "Remember when the streetcar tracks ran down this street?"

"Sure do. It was called 'the interurban.' Everyone rode the streetcar into town. We would shop Halliburton's and John A. Brown and we'd go into Harry Katz drug store for a cherry coke."

I laughed. "The first joke I ever remember was about that drug store. 'Did you hear about the two ladies in fur coats walking down the street? All of a sudden they turned into Harry Katz.'" To groans and laughter, we turned the corner into Twenty-first Street. We drove slowly down the block, and Don said, "There it is. That's the house we lived in when we moved from the house on Twenty-third Street. It was Mrs. Eberhardt's house. It was divided into four apartments. Oh my gosh, look at it."

Carolyn stopped the car, and Don snapped a picture. The building was a great rectangular box still decorated for Christmas. Identical green wreaths hung in all the upstairs windows, and green garlands were suspended from the rain gutter by red bows across the width of the house.

"They've torn off the porch and redone the front. And someone painted it yellow."

"I'm surprised this neighborhood has been kept up. These houses were all built in the late twenties or early thirties."

"I remember Janet." Oh Lord, yes. We all remembered Janet.

*O*KLAHOMA CITY–1937

*T*hat summer, at precisely four o'clock in the afternoon, our next door neighbor's screen door would open with a bang, and a wet and very naked four-year-old would propel herself across the porch and down the steps. Little Janet, having just emerged from her daily bath, would run down our street, her fat little legs churning, her sweating and harried mother in hot pursuit. Everyone stopped whatever they were doing to watch the drama. Kids giggled and screeched. "There goes Janet." Women raised their eyebrows in disapproval.

"I think it's just awful. I can understand how it could have happened the first time, but now she's letting that child become the scandal of the neighborhood. What kind of a mother would allow her child to expose herself for all to see?" Our mother was something of a prude. Our father was not.

"There's not much there to see. I think it's funny."

Mother's mouth tightened in disdain. "Oh, you would."

Not only did Janet run naked in the streets. She also ate caterpillars. To the horror and delight of the neighborhood children she would pick up a fuzzy little creature, open her mouth and stick out her tongue. She would place the wriggling worm on the tip end. By that time, every child in her audience was bug-eyed and horrified. As the creature crawled toward her mouth, Janet would draw him in, and with two sickening crunches of her teeth and a great gulp, she would swallow him.

Screams erupted from the children, prompting mothers from three houses away to drop their dish towels and run toward our back yard.

"What in the name of heavenly glory?"

"Janet ate a caterpillar."

"Oooooo, I'm going to be sick."

"Did you see that? It was all green and gooshy."

Our mother was the one in charge. "Oh, for goodness sake. Janet, go home this instant and tell your mother to wash your mouth out with soap." This curative was ordinarily reserved for children who took the Lord's name in vain, but this was an emergency. "The rest of you boys and girls go on about your business. She just does these things to get attention. Now, go on and play." With a shudder, she turned and went back to her kitchen. We children were both repelled and fascinated. "Oooooo, a caterpillar! I wonder what one tastes like?"

$\mathcal{O}$KLAHOMA CITY–1993

$\mathcal{I}$ wonder whatever happened to Janet?"

Carolyn turned the key in the ignition. "I don't know. I hope by now she can keep her clothes on and her diet has improved. Where to, now?"

"Go on up to Twenty-third Street, and let's go by Trinity."

"Trinity, it is."

Within minutes, we were parked across the street from the old church, and Don was busy with his camera. "What have they done to the front of it? Ann, when did they change it?"

"I don't remember what year it was they widened the street and put in the new entrance."

The building looked foreshortened. When we were members in the '40s, there was a flight of steep concrete steps bisected by an iron handrail. The steps led through ionic columns through heavy doors into the foyer of the sanctuary. Now the steps, as we had known them, were gone. In their place was a walled red brick platform with steps, not up the front, but on either side.

"I see they have taken down their neon sign, too."

"Oh, that's been down for years."

"Can you imagine a neon sign in front of a church?"

"They must have put that up when neon was new. I can see that thing now, changing from an open Bible to 'We Preach Christ.' It was blue and orange and yellow. How tacky."

"I remember when I was a little girl, I would be in the back seat on the way to church on Sunday nights. I can remember being tired, but when we got in sight of the church I would try to be the first one to see the neon sign. And, by the way, eight o'clock on Sunday night was the holy hour. No one thought to schedule for the convenience of young families."

"This place is full of ghosts."

OKLAHOMA CITY—1944

We went to Trinity Baptist Church. Daddy was a deacon and both mama and daddy taught the young married people in Sunday School. We started going there when mama and daddy got married; daddy drove by it and said, "That's where we're going to church." They joined the next Sunday–daddy by letter from the First Baptist Church in Carnegie. Mama joined on statement of faith, and then Dr. Harvey baptized her the next week. We kids didn't join the church, because we were not yet old enough to accept Jesus as our personal Savior.

My earliest memory was being handed over the double Dutch door of the nursery by my father into the waiting arms of Mrs. Lancaster or Mrs. Meyers. I remember the blue snow suit I wore with leggings that zipped up the sides, the baby beds, and the toys. I remember my playmate–Ray Miles Rush. He and I were in a wedding together. I was the flower girl. I wore a floor length turquoise organdy dress. He was the ring bearer and wore a tux.

I remember Billy McLain's fifth birthday party. His mother had invited only little boys, but Billy wouldn't have his party until I got there. His daddy took my picture in front of their white garage doors. I was shy, but I smiled for the camera. That day, I wore a maroon cotton dress with a white pique collar edged in eyelet. There were little white buttons down the front. My maroon and white socks matched my dress. I had on white high-topped shoes that were scuffed at the toes. Mother didn't have time to polish them before the party. On the following Monday, Mrs. McLain called my mother and told her that Billy was dead. He died on the operating table having his tonsils out. I remember his daddy standing in prayer meeting the next Wednesday night with tears streaming down his face, reading what David said when Bathsheba's son died: "My son cannot come to me, but I will go to him." The church family was devastated by Billy's death.

My best friend was Marilyn Fuller. She was beautiful and good and fun. Once when we were at her house, she showed me how to make a "Tom Collins." We made it with ginger ale, lemon juice, and sugar. I had no idea that any other ingredient might be required. We sipped our drinks from her mother's crystal iced tea glasses. We felt like movie stars. I also remember Carol Ann Thompson, and Dorothy Jean Reed. Dorothy Jean's birthday was in the summer, and her mother let her have slumber parties. We slept not at all, and after midnight, we would go for a walk in our pajamas around her neighborhood. We were all Trinity kids.

In Sunday School, after you were too old for the nursery, you became a Beginner (ages 4-5), a Primary (ages 6,7,8) and then a Junior (ages 9-11). My Beginner teacher was a sweet-faced woman named Margaret Crowder; my primary teacher was Jewel Kirkpatrick. These dear women dedicated them-selves to the religious education of children.

On Sunday nights we went to Story Hour. Every week we sang:

"Every Sunday evening
To the church we go,
To the happy story hour,
And we love it so.
The story hour, the story hour,
The happy story hour.
We sing and pray and listen well
At the happy story hour."

In addition to story hour and Sunday School, we went to children's church where Mrs. Lina Beck Hoppell, a former missionary, presented object lessons to a roomful of children sitting in rows. We were attentive to her every word. Once she peeled an already sliced banana before our very eyes. How did she do that? I don't remember the spiritual lesson she was trying to impart, but I remember the sliced banana. She presented us the plan of salvation using colors: black for sin, red for the shed blood of Jesus, white for your heart after it had been washed in the blood.

We sang with great gusto:

The B-I-B-L-E,

Oh, that's the book for me.

I stand alone on the word of God,

The B-I-B-L-E.

On the word "stand" we would all stomp our feet in unison, sounding like the U. S. Cavalry.

By the age of seven, although I hadn't had time to do too much sinning, I knew I needed Jesus as my Savior. I well remember the Sunday night I pulled at my mother's hand at the invitation hymn saying, "I want to go down front." Mama told me we'd talk about it, and talk we did. All that next week, I was quizzed. I could answer all the questions about Jesus dying on the cross for me. The next Saturday, I walked to church and met Mrs. Hoppell who had me pray the sinner's prayer: "Dear God, I know that I am a sinner. I am truly sorry and I repent of my sins. I open my heart and ask Jesus to come in and save me from my sin and give me eternal life. Amen."

The next Sunday night, at invitation time, the congregation sang,

"Just as I am without one plea,

But that Thy blood was shed for me,

And that Thou bidst me come to Thee,

Oh, Lamb of God, I come. I come."

I did go down front at that invitation, professed my childish faith in the Lord Jesus, and a few weeks later, R.C. Miller, our interim pastor, baptized me.

My mama told me that I should think of Jesus on the cross while I was going through the baptism. I did think of Jesus as the pastor said, "Because of your profession of faith in the Lord Jesus, and because you believe he died to save you from your sins, I baptize you, my little sister, in the name of the Father, the Son and the Holy Ghost. Amen." He dipped me beneath the water while I held my nose, and I heard the words, "We are buried with Christ through baptism, and we are raised to walk in Eunice of life." I always wondered who Eunice was.

During the war years when we worshiped in the sanctuary, I was allowed to draw on the church bulletin. I often drew Dr. Harvey, our pastor at that time, as a stick figure, one arm pointing to heaven and the other pointing down to hell. He preached a lot from Revelation and said that Hitler was the antichrist. I knew it was wrong to hate, but I hated Hitler with all my little-girl heart. I used to fantasize about killing him. I knew that if we could just get rid of him there wouldn't be anymore trouble in the world ever.

After I had been baptized, I often wished the pastor would ask the people who believed in Jesus to stand on one side of the room, and the people who did not believe to stand on the other. That way everyone would know who was, and who was not, a believer. I, of course, would be standing with the saints. I had not yet learned about spiritual pride.

The pulpit in our sanctuary was in the middle of the stage, the choir behind it. When the young men began to volunteer for military service, and others were drafted, someone thought it might be a good idea to keep the congregation aware of our boys. On both sides of the platform, black, shiny plaques were secured to the wall with tiny screws. On each plaque was a photograph of a young man in uniform. These were our kids who had gone out from Trinity. Every Sunday we prayed for our boys. Every Sunday, gold and silver stars appeared beside the photographs. Gold stars meant that someone had been killed in combat. Silver stars were for the wounded. Our church was full every Sunday of people who had someone overseas. It was a time of great anxiety and great sorrow.

I remember, one Sunday, one of our boys was home on furlough. He stood in the pulpit and gave his testimony. He was a bomber pilot. I remember he said, "If God knows when a sparrow falls, I figure he can't miss a B-29." People quoted him for weeks. We prayed hard for our boys. I couldn't understand why there were so many gold stars on our plaques. Why didn't God do something to save our boys? I didn't understand why God didn't swoop down and end the war.

OKLAHOMA CITY–1993

We stood in front of the church remembering the people that we had known there—Dr. Yearby, our dear pastor who had come to us after Dr. Harvey, and Mr. Bates the Sunday School Superintendent. He ran that Sunday School like it was the United States Army.

"If you can't come to Wednesday night teachers' meeting, I don't want you teaching a class." He laid down the rules. For an hour every Wednesday evening downstairs in the fellowship hall, Mr. Bates taught teachers how to teach. Mother and daddy both taught classes. They wouldn't have missed a teachers meeting for anything in the world. It was a top priority.

"Begin studying your lesson on Monday. Read the scripture. Read the comments in the teachers' quarterly. Always find a way to present the plan of salvation. You never know who might be in your class who has never accepted Christ as personal Savior."

Our mother took copious notes. She taught the young married women's class, and daddy taught their husbands. His class dwindled because his young men were called into military service. The young wives became a support group for each other.

Oh, those Sunday School classes! Billie Burnside was in mother's class. She had a little girl named Judy, a baby boy named J.D., and a husband named Ed. Billie, in spite of two pregnancies, looked like a malnourished twelve-year-old boy. She was skinny as a rail and flat as a board. One night the classes met at our house for a tacky party. They came dressed like the rag picker's child. Sam Flood wore farmer's overalls complete with patches. Betty Saxon dressed as a hooker. She wore fishnet stockings and carried an unlit cigar. Great laughter greeted her entrance.

Then Billie came strutting in and announced: "Hey, everyone! Can you tell? I've gained three pounds." Cheers erupted from the party goers.

"Hey, Ed," someone shouted. "Can you tell any difference in her bosoms?"

Ed grinned. "Sure can. One is the size of a pea, and the other is a little bitty thing."

At one party, they decided to have a contest and award a prize for the best looking legs. All the men rolled up their pants legs and stood behind a blanket. Two women held the blanket so the men were hidden from the knees up. The rest of the women served as the panel of judges. What they saw from floor to blanket's edge was a collection of hairy male legs. There was much comparison and irreverent commentary. After considerable deliberation and some argument, daddy won the prize. I don't remember what he won.

During the war, everything was rationed to civilians. It

was impossible to get sugar, butter, meat, gasoline, nylons, shoes. Everything went to our servicemen. Once, Luther "Pete" Peterson, who worked at Wilson's Meat Packing Company, wangled a bunch of T-bones and the two Sunday School classes met at our house for a steak fry. Mother had put us to bed early to get us out of the way of the adults. I'll never forget Pete's coming into our bedroom with two plates piled with french fries and steaks. Carolyn and I sat up in bed and ate every bite.

We associated so many memories with Trinity. It was here that I first saw Bob Brown when he came back from Korea. He and my brother had been best friends since they were twelve. Donald and Bob went to Boy Scouts together. They had gone hunting together. Once, by mistake, my brother shot a hole in the floorboard of Bob's dad's car. When I saw Bob on the church steps, I was back in Oklahoma for my sixteenth summer. Bob told me he would be stationed at Quantico, just down the road from Alexandria where we lived. He asked about Donald, of course. He asked for our phone number and promised to call when I got back home to Virginia. Later, he came to visit, and to eat our mother's cooking. It wasn't long after, that he married my sister.

My sixteenth summer was the summer I stayed with Ann and Sam. My new girl friends all sang in Gene Bartlett's triple trio—the Trinity Trebles. Gene was the beloved Minister of Music at Trinity who, years later, was Mr. Music for all the Baptist churches across Oklahoma. He led the music at Falls Creek Baptist Assembly that year when we went on a youth retreat. My Aunt Ann was a sponsor. The young people ran in gangs. No one went steady. No one had to have a date. We just studied and played and laughed and flirted. What a great time. It was the summer I pitched nine innings of a softball game at Falls Creek, and when our team won, the boys carried me down to the creek and threw me in. I was so tired, I sank to the bottom, and Jay jumped in and pulled me out. How chivalrous of him! What a hunk! It was the summer I fell in love with Jay Chance. Most of the girls did at one time or another. He was tall, athletic, blonde and blue-eyed, and the best Christian of us all. He was no fanatic, however. That was the summer Jay kissed me goodnight, knocked three milk bottles off Ann's front porch, and fell into a rose bush.

I chuckled softly to myself. "Do you remember when Jay Chance kissed me and fell into your rose bush?" I asked Ann.

"No, but I remember Falls Creek and trying to keep up with that bunch of kids. I have never been so worn out as I was the week after Falls Creek. In some ways, it seems like yesterday. And in some ways, it seems a hundred years ago."

When we piled back into Carolyn's Lincoln to finish our sentimental journey, we drove by our old elementary school, where Carolyn started to kindergarten. Carolyn started to kindergarten in September after her fourth birthday in May. Before the first day of school, daddy showed her how to walk to school and which landmarks to look for. The first day of school, without her being aware of it, he followed her in his car to make sure she didn't get lost. She walked from the capitol building on Twenty third Street (also Highway 66), all the way to Walker—a total of some fourteen city blocks–just over a mile. She crossed Twenty-third at the light and walked the three blocks to Woodrow Wilson Elementary School. Barely four years old, that child walked that distance alone, to and from school every day for the school year. No one thought she might be kidnapped, raped, or murdered. What were our parents thinking?

When I started kindergarten there, I began in January,

just as I turned five. I was enrolled in the afternoon session. Daddy came home from work that day to eat lunch and take me to school. He took me into the room, deposited me on the floor, and left me. I cried. That was the second time he'd pulled that trick on me. He never was very good at preparing me in advance for new experiences, but I had it easier than Carolyn did. Although, the next day, and for the rest of the semester, I walked alone as well. By that time, we had moved to Twenty-fifth Street, and I only had to walk seven blocks. I suppose in those days there was no such thing as a mom who acted as chauffeur, but in light of what happened to the Lindberg baby, it was not simply a more innocent time when bad things didn't happen to children. At any rate, all the children we knew walked wherever they went. We certainly did. Mother did not know how to drive a car, and daddy wasn't about to relinquish his vehicle for anything as mundane as taking children to school. It did not even occur to him that he should drive my mother to the grocery store. I remember that she would carry groceries in her arms the five city blocks from the store to our house.

Oklahoma City–1941

I wanted to go about doing good. I knew that if I could do good, I would ingratiate myself with Miss Madison, my first grade teacher at Woodrow Wilson Elementary School, and all the children would be my friends. I tried to think of some great virtuous deed that would accomplish my goal. Then I had it. When all the other children were on the playground, I would sneak back into the classroom and perform some grand, selfless, act of good. We all used big, fat pencils. Our chubby little hands grasped them and with them, we formed our ABCs. I noticed that some children did not keep their pencils sharpened. I would perform an act of kindness and sharpen those pencils, saving my fellow students the trouble. While they were on the playground playing "Red Rover, Red Rover," I would give up my playtime, make the great sacrifice, and do that good thing. I felt noble even as I thought of it.

On Wednesday, when everyone was at recess, I slipped back into the classroom. Children had left their pencils in the horizontal slot cut across the upper edge of their wooden desk tops. I began by sharpening one pencil and putting it back where I found it, but this proved too slow. I decided to expedite the process. I gathered all the pencils in a pile and began to sharpen them. I basked in my own virtue. How delighted everyone would be with their pencils, and with my generous gift of time and effort.

"That's okay," I would say. "I was glad to do it for you. You are my friends."

I stood at the window for perhaps ten minutes trying to complete my task before the others returned. Unfortunately, I didn't remember which pencil belonged on which desk. The children began to arrive and Miss Madison, too, returned from her break.

I turned to face the children. "I sharpened all the pencils. You will have to come and find yours, because I don't remember where I got them." Children began to complain.

"I can't find my pencil."

"This isn't my pencil. Mine is longer than this."

"My pencil was red. This one is blue."

"This isn't my pencil. Mine doesn't have teeth marks on it." There was grand confusion. I was beginning to feel fear. This was not the scenario I had envisioned.

Miss Madison was less than thrilled. "Roberta, you must keep your hands off other people's things. This is not good. Look what has happened here. I am very unhappy with you."

How could all of my good intentions have produced such terrible results? Instead of glowing in the praise of others, I was suffering shame and humiliation under their negative opinion of me.

Tears pooled in my eyes. "I didn't mean to."

Miss Madison nodded. "I'm sure you didn't, but you did it anyway. You'll need to stand in the corner."

I hung my head in shame: a good girl gone wrong. It was true. I had tried so hard to be good. I would just have to try harder. I had not yet heard the phrase, "She's more to be pitied than censured." I was getting pity from no one but myself. The complaints about the pencils lasted all through that day. Life is hard, and it's miserable when you are six years old and so dreadfully misunderstood.

$\mathcal{O}$KLAHOMA–1993

$\mathcal{W}$e took I-40 out of the City and when we got to Highway 58, we turned south toward Carnegie. It was January in Oklahoma where "the wind comes sweeping down the plain." The wind always blows in Oklahoma. In summer, it's hot and dry. On that day, it was cold and bone-chilling. The sun cast feeble rays of light, but no warmth. To my eyes, accustomed to the tall trees in the hilly woodlands of Virginia, the scrubby little trees, permanently bent by perpetual wind, were pygmies. Don laughed. "When people ask me where Carnegie is, I always tell them it's between Fort Cobb and Gotebo."

"Oh, that's helpful." The time passed in pleasant chatter. The all-but-silent motor of the Lincoln purred effortlessly as the miles rolled under us.

"I sure could get used to this car." I could not help but compare this mammoth to the Honda Civic I drove at home. "If I parked my car beside yours, Carolyn, it would look like yours had given birth."

Carolyn smiled. "I love my Lincoln. It's prettier than this one. It's my color—baby blue. I told the dealer I would not buy the car if I couldn't get it in blue. I tell you, he hopped around to find the one I wanted. My car has wonderful features. It's just like this one except for the color. It tells how much fuel you have used and how much farther you can go on what's in the tank. It talks out loud to you if you have left your keys in the ignition or the door isn't shut all the way. The door unlocks with a little gizmo I carry on my key chain. The lights go off automatically. I paid more for that car than we paid for our first house. And it's a lot more luxurious than that first house. That's for sure. I do love my Lincoln. Yessir! It cost more than our first house."

We passed farmland and grain elevators, houses and barns, and fallow fields. Soon we crossed over the Washita River bridge. My brother grinned. "That's 'WASH-ih-taw' with the accent on the first syllable. When I was a kid I called it 'Wa-SHIT-tuh' until Granddad McGregor corrected me. 'That's 'WASH-ih-taw,' son,' he told me. 'Watch your mouth.'"

"We're coming into Carnegie. What do you want to see first? Not that there's that much to see." Carolyn swung onto Main Street. It was practically deserted. "I remember when everyone came to town on Saturday."

"Well, maybe folks have sense enough to stay in out of

the wind."

"Go on down to the church," Don instructed. "It's down beyond the flag pole."

"I remember where it is."

We passed a drug store, a flower shop, and a movie theater which appeared to be closed down. We drove by the offices of *The Carnegie Herald.* On the corner was an "antique" shop, its windows cluttered with junk. I made a mental note that I would like to go in there and see if I could find depression glass.

I spoke up from the back seat. "Sometimes churches have photographs of all their former pastors lined up on a wall. Maybe we can find a picture of our grandfather."

Carolyn parked against the curb. We scrambled out of the car. "Ann, are you okay?"

"Yes, I'm fine. Just give me a hand." Don helped her out of the back seat. We walked to the church and up the concrete steps that led to the sanctuary, pulling our coats more tightly around us against the wind. The church had been recently renovated. The front doors were now made of heavy glass and they were locked against intruders. We stood with noses flattened against the panes, four old pilgrims on a sentimental journey.

"What can you see?"

"Nothing much." Don shifted from one door to the other. "I sure can't see any photographs."

"May I help you? Would you like to go inside? I have a key." We had not heard her approach, so intent were we on our quest. "I'm Ernestine Hayworth. I'll be glad to show you around."

"Oh how nice. Yes, we'd love to. I'm Carolyn Brown. This is my sister, Roberta Damon and our aunt, Ann Greer.

And this is our brother, Don McBride. We lived in Carnegie when we were small children, and our grandfather was pastor of this church years ago."

"Well, you probably won't recognize much now. We have just finished a renovation of our sanctuary, but you are welcome to come in." She led us on a tour of the church. The sanctuary was new beyond recognition. The only thing Don remembered was the communion table. Made of oak, it was unadorned except for the words carved into the front panel: "In remembrance of me." "I'm sure that's the communion table that was here when our grandfather was pastor back in the twenties."

"I expect so. It's about the only thing that has remained, I'm afraid."

Suddenly, Ann said to me, "I wonder if Mrs. Anderson is still living. Ask her if she knows a Mrs. Anderson. She took care of you when you were a baby."

I turned to our tour guide. "Mrs. Hayworth, do you know a Mrs. Anderson?"

"Do you mean May Anderson?"

"I don't know her first name. But she took care of me when I was a baby."

"Oh, you mean May Anderson. Yes, I know her."

"My goodness. How old is she?"

"She's ninety."

"Is she alert?"

"Yes, and she still lives in her own home. I can take you there if you like."

"Oh, we'd like that, thank you."

As we stepped outside the church, Carolyn discovered she had locked her keys in the car. Carolyn and Don stayed with the car while Mrs. Hayworth took Ann and me in her own car over to Mrs. Anderson's house. She let us out and then went back to help Carolyn and Don.

The house was small and neat–a white frame house with a back stoop. I stepped up on the small back porch and knocked at the kitchen door. A tiny, fragile, slightly bent, woman answered. I was aware that she came barely to my chin.

"Mrs. Anderson?"

"Yes?"

"It's Roberta."

"Oh, honey." Her eyes filled with tears. "I didn't think God was going to let me live long enough ever to see you again. Come in."

Ann and I stepped into her kitchen.

"Come on in the front room." We sat facing each other. She looked at me and began, "You were born January 19, 1935."

"Yes."

"You weighed seven pounds, eleven ounces."

"I never knew that."

"Your mother never held you because she was so sick."

"I didn't know that. All I know is that I stayed in the hospital for the first six months of my life and then daddy took me home. I know he remarried when I was two and..." I looked at her. She was shaking her head 'no.'

"What?"

"You stayed in the hospital for six weeks, not six months. Your mother died on a Friday and she was buried on a Sunday. Your daddy came to me and said, 'Mrs. Anderson, I want you to take the baby.' So on Monday morning, Melford and I went down to the hospital and got you. And your daddy didn't get married two years after your mother's death. He got married seven months after she died."

I felt like someone had hit me hard in the stomach.

"Your grandfather was my pastor and your grandmother was the best Christian I ever knew."

We heard Carolyn and Don knocking on the back door. Mrs. Anderson went to let them in. "I'm Carolyn," I heard her say. And Mrs. Anderson's response, "Honey, I've loved you all your life. Come in." As they came into the living room, I turned to them, ashen-faced and shaken. "She knew our Granddad McGregor. He was her pastor. And she knew our mother." We all sat stunned. Here was the living link to our birth mother. And we had never heard of her before this moment. Then the questions tumbled out, one over another.

*M*ARCH–1935

*M*ay went with Melford down to the hospital. Melford had a tooth that was killing him and May had finally told him he had to have the dentist look at it. The 'dental office' consisted of an old dentist chair they had set up in a windowless store room that also held a baby bed and shelves stocked with medicines. May was surprised to find a crying baby in the crib. The infant's arm was twisted under her, so May reached down to make the child more comfortable.

"What are you doing? You don't come in here and touch a patient." It was a very angry nurse.

"I'm sorry. The baby was crying. I just got her arm out from under her. This is Keith McBride's baby. I know Keith well." May was taken aback by the woman's aggressive attitude.

"I don't care what you were doing or who you think you

know. Just don't touch that child. That baby is always crying. We call her the 'cry baby.' No one can get her to stop. But you better just step back. That baby is not your business."

Melford looked at the baby and then at the nurse. "You probably don't know me," he said. "I'm the night watchman for Carnegie. It breaks my heart to go by here at night and hear this child cry. My wife was just trying to help."

"I do wish you people would just mind your own business." She hurried out, leaving May embarrassed and Melford angry.

"Don't pay her any mind, May. You did the right thing."

Don had come to the Andersons on Saturday. "Keith will be buried tomorrow. I don't know what I'm going to do about the baby. I don't know how to ask you this, but I'm wondering if you would take her, at least for the time being."

Melford and May didn't have to think about it. "Yes, of course. We'd love to take the baby." May's heart leapt at the thought.

Now it was Monday morning. May and Melford walked into the foyer of the hospital and stepped up to speak to the receptionist. "We're here to pick up the McBride baby. Her father has asked us to take her." She looked down her nose at them.

"Oh? We'll have to see about that." She went to find the doctor.

Dr. Taylor came to the front desk. He carried the infant in his arms and laid the baby in May's outstretched arms. "Don't love this baby. She's going to die within a week. It won't do for you to get too attached." May looked at the tiny little face, pale and pinched. She hugged the infant to her breast and, under her breath, she vowed, "This baby will not die."

CARNEGIE-1993

I helped May into her easy chair.

"Oh, honey, I took you home and took you off all the medicine they had been giving you. I knew a lady who lived down the way from me. She owned a Jersey cow. I contracted with her for a pint of milk in the morning and a pint of milk in the evening. And that's what I did. I gave that milk to you straight from that cow, and you thrived."

I thought of myself as an infant in a closed room in that hospital. No one picked me up. My mother never held me. "Failure to thrive" was a term no one had heard in 1935. But babies did turn their faces to the wall and die for lack of tender, loving care. They thought I was dying. I realized in that moment that I very likely would have died if this tiny lady had not come along and saved my life with her sheer determination—and that unpasteurized milk from a Jersey cow. And then the thought, "Oh, my gosh. Typhoid."

CARNEGIE-1935

I can't believe he would do this to us." Effie wept softly into her handkerchief. "Keith not gone a year yet, and he has already run off and gotten himself married. Everyone's talking about it. I can't hold my head up in Carnegie now. This whole town's buzzing. I'm just so humiliated."

R.K. cleared his throat. "Well, Effie, I know it's hard on you—on us, but he had those children to consider. Someone has to mother them now Keith is gone." His voice broke. "Poor little motherless tykes. I hope she is good to them. She is a Christian woman, Effie. That's my only hope."

"I can't believe a Christian woman would flaunt herself around a widower and lure him into marrying her. I just have to wonder if she is really saved. Oh, my poor grandbabies. My sweet Donald Keith and my dear little Carolyn. What will they do now that they have a stepmother? Oh, dear Lord, what kind of a man would kill our daughter to satisfy his own dark lusts and leave his poor children motherless?"

"Now, Effie, he didn't kill Keith on purpose. It's not like he choked her to death."

"I know that, but I do hold him responsible for her death. And now, I hold him responsible for getting married a bare seven months after she died. He could have just waited a decent interval. It's like he has no respect for the dead. It's like he didn't love Keith enough to grieve for her even a year. My poor daughter. Out of sight, out of mind. It's just so unfair. My darling lies in the Carnegie cemetery and he is in bed with that woman. I heard that her own brother won't even speak to her. What a hussy. I'd just like to scratch her eyes out, that's what."

"Now, Effie, you know what scripture says, 'Vengeance is mine, saith the Lord.' That's just not something you can fix. Let's hope they can provide a happy Christian home for the children. Come on. Get dressed. We're going to pay them a call."

"Oh, husband, I have such a headache. I just don't think my nerves can stand it."

R.K. prevailed and they bundled up against the November chill. He helped her into the passenger side of the old Ford and then slid behind the steering wheel. "Effie, I'll do the talking if this makes you nervous. Just pray as we go, and the Lord will give us strength."

As they drove the few blocks to Don's house, R.K. recalled that it was eight years ago that Don had come to him asking for Keith's hand. He certainly wasn't about to express his thoughts out loud to Effie. R.K. tried to keep from setting her off. Effie was delicate. His thoughts intruded. The memories persisted. Eight years. Keith in love was something to see. Keith a bride. Keith pregnant. Keith in labor. Keith loving those children. Keith struggling for breath with pneumonia—so weak after the third baby. Keith bleeding. Keith dying. He pushed the thought from his mind. "It's mighty cold out tonight. See you keep that blanket over you so you don't get a chill."

Effie pulled the wool blanket up to her chin. "It's just such a scandal. I just have to wonder what went on in that house. That woman was in that house all during the week while Don was working in Oklahoma City—abandoning our babies, mind you, and coming home only on the weekends. I'd just like to know what happened when he got home. That's what I'd like to know. Why, while our girl was dying in that hospital, I just wonder what was going on behind her back. It just seems to me something was going on. You just don't up and get married to someone unless you know them mighty well."

"Now, Effie, that's just the talk that's going around. You just can't listen to that kind of talk. I don't think Don would do such a thing."

"Well, you may not think he would do it, but he did do it. I've got my suspicions."

"Effie, that's beauty parlor talk, and you know it."

"I know no such thing." Her eyes were red and swollen. Effie had a headache.

They turned off the pavement of Main Street onto the

dirt of East Third. Three houses from the corner they pulled up in front of what had been Don and Keith's small frame home. "Now, Effie," R.K. warned as he stepped out of the car, "Watch your mouth."

"Oh, Lord, help us in our time of need." Effie sent the quick prayer heavenward as she got out of her side. Together they walked up the front walkway. R.K. knocked.

Don came to the door. "Well, look who's here." The children, bathed and in pajamas, squealed in delight. "Papa and Nana." R.K. picked Donald up and gave him a bear hug. Carolyn clung to Effie's knees. Effie wiped her tears and hugged her girl. "Oh, I've missed you so much. Look at you. What a big girl you are."

Don took their coats and invited them to sit down. "Oh, we can't stay long. We leave to go back to our church field tomorrow morning early. We're just in town to see the children." R.K. pulled Donald up on the couch beside him.

"Yes," Effie added emphatically, "And to visit Keith's grave." There was an awkward momentary silence. The air was thick between them with unspoken accusation.

Don nodded. "Let me just get Mary Lou in here. You will like her." He stepped into the hallway that led to the kitchen.

Effie sniffed and murmured, "I already don't like her."

R.K. suddenly began to sing a song about a man that kept falling off his bicycle. It made the children laugh.

Don appeared nervous and Mary Lou reluctant as they stepped into the living room. She was almost as tall as her new husband. She was nothing like Keith at all. This one was slim with dark hair and beautiful olive skin. She had a pronounced widow's peak that defined large gray eyes.

"I've put the kettle on for tea. It won't take but a few

minutes." Her speech was pure East Tennessee.

Effie nodded and thought, "A hillbilly. Don has gone and married a hillbilly. Oh, my poor babies."

R.K. spoke. "Thank you kindly, Miss Mary Lou. A cup of tea would go good on a night like this. We were just wondering if you would let these children come and visit us again next summer. We would love to have them for the whole summer if that's all right with you, Don."

"Would you kids like to go visit your Papa and Nana next summer?"

"Yes," squealed Donald with delight. "Yes," echoed Carolyn, not to be left out.

"When is summer?" Donald asked.

"Not for a long time, I'm afraid. But when it starts getting warm outside and it's time to plant corn, why, we'll just come get you and take you home with us."

"Yippeee. Let's plant corn tonight."

"Not tonight, pal. It's time for you two to go to bed." Don reached for the boy. "It's way past bedtime."

Effie stood. "Oh, Don, let me put them to bed. I want to pray with them."

"Of course, Effie." She carried Carolyn and led Donald by the hand into their bedroom.

R.K. took advantage of Effie's absence. "We wish you well. You must know that we hold no animosity in our hearts toward you. Miss Mary Lou, there is a lot of ugly talk around town about your marriage to Don. Don't pay it any mind. Half the people are saying you all got married too quick. The other half are saying Don needed a wife bad. Our concern is for the children. We would like to see them as often as we can. The best thing for us is to have them in the summers. This past summer we all did just fine together.

We take good care of them, so you don't have to worry about that. We just don't want the children to forget us or their mother." He choked, wiped his eyes with the back of his hand, and cleared his throat. "How do you feel about that?"

"We don't have any desire to keep the children from you." Don set his cup of tea on the table beside his chair. "We've all been through a lot and it's time now to just get on with our lives."

Mary Lou spoke softly, "Brother McGregor, I'm sorry for your loss. I promise to keep these children clean and well-fed. I've taken care of many a child in my day."

Don nodded. "Mary Lou took care of her brothers and sisters after her mother died, and she was a school teacher, and now she's a nurse." He enumerated her qualifications as if she were a job applicant. "She's a wonderful cook. She's got these kids cleaning their plates."

R.K. nodded his thanks. "The Lord bless you, dear lady."

Effie came back into the room. "They are sleeping. Oh, my poor little motherless babies. What will become of them?"

Don felt rather than saw Mary Lou's mouth tighten and her right eyebrow rise. He hoped she would not say anything. He was aware of how hard she had worked. She had cooked and cleaned and scrubbed and looked after the children. He knew she thought it was unhealthy to encourage them to dwell on their mother's death.

R.K. stood. "Don, we need to be getting on. If you'll get our coats."

"I'll get them."

Mary Lou stepped into the bedroom and brought the heavy wool garments. As they were bundling up against the cold night air, R.K. suddenly asked, "What about the baby?"

"She's still over at Melford and May Anderson's house.

She seems to be doing fine. Mrs. Anderson takes good care of her. They are talking about adopting her. I don't know, yet. The baby has never known anything but them. I just don't know what we'll do."

Effie shook her head sadly, "That child cost Keith her life."

"Well, come on, Effie. We need to get some sleep before our trip tomorrow." They said their good-byes. As they got back into their car, R.K. commented, "Now, Effie, that wasn't so bad. Was it?"

"Oh, my precious babies. And that woman is using Keith's things. Her tea cups, her spoons. She's sleeping in Keith's bed. She's sleeping with Keith's husband. She takes care of Keith's children. Oh, the children. What will become of them?"

"Summer is coming, Effie. We can have them all summer long."

CARNEGIE/OKLAHOMA CITY–1935

Carnegie, Oklahoma
April 2, 1935
Dear Mr. McBride,

Your children are adjusting quite well. They talk about their mother sometimes. They ask where you are, particularly at bedtime. I tell them you are working and will be home at the end of the week. I assure them that I'll be near if they need me during the night. Donald is old enough to count the days until you come home again. He plays well with his friends in the neighborhood. He understands he must mind me. Carolyn is a very stubborn child. She holds her breath and falls on the floor when things don't go to suit. I am a very strong believer in discipline. Children cannot be allowed to have the upper hand. I keep these children on a schedule. I believe it is best for them. If you have any instructions for me, please let me know. I shall try to comply.

Sincerely,

Mary Lou Patterson

Oklahoma City

April 5, 1935

Dear Miss Patterson,

Thank you for your letter about the children. I should be back in Carnegie by Friday night. I hope you get this note before I get there. I am grateful to you for what you are doing for my children. I don't know yet what I will do in the future about them or about my work. For the present, I feel they are getting from you the care and attention they need.

Gratefully,

Don O. McBride

Carnegie, Oklahoma

May 5, 1935

Dear Don,

We are having a pretty good week. I am concerned that both children are still wetting the bed. I have put the step stool from the back porch in the kitchen in front of the sink so they can get their own drinks of water. I do not allow them to have water after four in afternoon. You may have noticed that the children will refuse to eat their dinner and then, as soon as everything is put away, they will ask for bread and butter and sugar. I will not allow this. If they refuse to eat their dinner, they will just have to go hungry until the next meal. They will begin to eat what is put before them. I hope all of this meets with your approval. I am doing this for their own good. I look forward to seeing you on Saturday.

Best,

Mary Lou

Oklahoma City
May 8, 1935
Dear Mary Lou,

Thanks for the news about the children. You really are getting things under control.

Of course, I approve. The children's mother was a very sweet girl, but she didn't know how to keep a clean house or control the children. There was many a night during my marriage that I stayed late downtown so as to avoid the chaos. I'm afraid the grandparents have spoiled them, too, and that hasn't helped. It is really wonderful to come home on the weekends to a clean house and children who are eating well and are so well cared for. You are doing a wonderful job. I could get used to this. I haven't eaten so well since my mother cooked for me when I was a kid. You are a wonderful person. See you Saturday.

Cordially,

Don

Carnegie, Oklahoma
June 3, 1935
Dear Don,

Carolyn is down for a nap and Donald is playing outside with Billy. Today is my birthday, so I thought I would write you a letter as a gift to myself. Coming to Carnegie was not an easy decision for me. I was a surgical nurse at the hospital in Knoxville, but I came out here because my brother, my Aunt Addie, and my Uncle John are here. I don't know why things happen the way they do. Maybe God has a plan. I saw Mrs. Anderson and the baby downtown this morning. She is getting fat–the baby, not Mrs. Anderson. I feel that people are making comments behind my back. Today, a woman stopped me on the street and said, "And how are the motherless children and how is Mr. McBride?" I said, "The children are fine, and as far as I know, Mr. McBride is fine, too." I guess you can't stop folks from talking. Well, it is time for me to get supper on. As soon as the McGregors come to get the children, I'll move back into the nurse's quarters at the hospital.

Take care,
Mary Lou

Oklahoma City
June 6, 1935

You are not going to believe this, but I had a birthday on June 1. So, happy birthday to you and happy birthday to me. Isn't that something? I am relieved that the children are doing so well. I know it is not easy for you. When I am home on the weekends, it is all I can do to keep up with those two–and I don't have to cook. Thanks for leaving the ice box full of food for us. I am amazed at how the children are eating. They are just like little pigs. The McGregors plan to be there to pick the children up for the summer on Thursday. I am glad you saw the baby. I still don't know what to do with her. The Andersons really want to adopt her, and I am more and more inclined to let them have her. She is happy there, and they love her. She would never know the difference. Don't be bothered about what people say. We just have to live our lives and if people don't like it they can stick their noses into the business of someone else. I do take care. You take care, too.

Fondly,

Don

Carnegie, Oklahoma

July 2, 1935

Dear Don,

It is much too soon for you to be thinking of me in that way. I don't know what to say to you except that I feel I must be honest with you. I get letters from a man in Tennessee. He lost his wife some years ago, and he has a little boy. He has asked me to marry him. I thought maybe I would, but then you came into the picture. I am so torn. I don't know what I will tell him. He is not pressuring me for an answer. I know that he needs me, and I already love his son. I don't tell you this to upset you. I just want to be honest with you. I do think that your loss is too recent for you to be thinking about being in love again. I will ask you not to pressure me. Please give me time to think.

Thinking of you,

Mary Lou

Oklahoma City

July 6, 1935

Dearest Mary Lou,

I am trying not to pressure you. I went to a fireworks display over the 4th. It was quite a show. It was nothing compared to what happens in my heart when I think of you. Don't pay any attention to that fellow in Tennessee. He doesn't need you half as much as I do. You are good and beautiful. I'm having trouble sleeping at night.

Love,

Don

Carnegie, Oklahoma

August 2, 1935

My dear Don,

Things are moving so fast. I want you to know that today I wrote to my friend in Tennessee and told him I cannot marry him. It was sad to write the letter and I know he and Tommy will be sad to get that news, but I feel it is the right thing. My sister, Ann, is in Carnegie for a visit. I told her I had made up my mind. She approves. She may be the only one. Do you know what it's going to be like around here when people in Carnegie hear that we are getting married? My brother, Ray, is angry at me. I got a lecture from him about how disrespectful I am. He doesn't approve of you, either. I guess we'll just ride out the storm together. Together with you is where I want to be.

Love always,

Mary Lou

Oklahoma City

August 5, 1935

My darling,

I can't wait to get back to Carnegie so I can hold you in my arms once again. We cannot pay attention to people who do not understand that love does not go by the calendar or the clock. Love just happens, and sometimes the time is not right. I have learned that you can't please everyone—not even everyone in your own family. I'm sorry your brother is mad at you. I would not want to cause a rift between the two of you. He'll get over it, and he and I will be friends one day. I only want your happiness, and I will work for the rest of my life to see that you are happy. We are going to make a great team. And we are going to be a great family. Take care, love, until I can take care of you.

I love you always,
Don

Carnegie, Oklahoma
September 3, 1935
My darling Don,

I can't believe how happy I am. I am living life as I always have, but I carry this secret in my heart. The children came home yesterday and asked where you were. It will be good when we can be a family. All of my hard work with them went down the drain over the summer. Their grandparents indulge their every whim. They came home unable to get their own glass of water. I will just have to get them back in shape. Anyway, in just a few weeks we will all be under one roof. You must be very careful with my heart. You own it, you know.

Just You,
Mary Lou

Oklahoma City
September 6, 1935
My darling girl,

You don't know what you have done to me. I haven't felt like this since I was a kid. I thought that my life was over, but you have given me hope and such happiness. I can't wait to get my hands on you. In just a few short weeks you will be

Mrs. Don McBride. How does that sound? It sounds great to me. We'll make our plans.

I love you forever,

Don

*G*UTHRIE, OKLAHOMA–
OCTOBER 5, 1935

*T*he first hint of fall was in the air. Indian summer had lasted through September. Now the leaves were beginning to turn. Don sat in the cramped little depot in Guthrie with the license in his pocket. He took the document out and read it over, pausing where the officiate would sign it. In this case it would be a justice of the peace. Glancing at the big clock over the clerk's counter, he felt nervous and slightly nauseous. He had heard the expression "butterflies in the stomach." That's how he felt. Would she be on the train from Carnegie? Of course, she would be. Why would he doubt?

He began to pace, unaware of his surroundings so focused was he on his own thoughts. "She may be, by golly, the best thing that has ever happened to me. Lord knows I need her. I hope the kids can adjust. Good thing they already know her. Has it only been seven months since Keith died? It seems like forever. People are going to talk something awful. I don't care. There is nothing sinful about matrimony." For one brief moment, he thought of a girl in Kansas and their son. Let's see, he would now be, my God–thirteen. For one moment, he remembered standing beside Bernice in her father's house, and that terrible ceremony. He couldn't remember her face. Then, he recalled another wedding in the Baptist parsonage in Carnegie with Keith glowing at his side. He managed to push those thoughts quickly from his mind.

Don was dressed in his only good suit. Camel-colored wool, it was freshly steam-cleaned and brushed. He had picked it up from the cleaners this morning. Careful as he dressed, he chose a crisply starched, white shirt and tied the ivory-colored silk tie. His wavy hair was parted smartly in the middle. He caught sight of his reflection in the glass of the depot window. He was of medium height. His electric blue eyes and square jaw were pure Irish. His chin jutted proudly as he struck a pose and smiled. "Good looking if I do say so, myself." He was a younger version of his father, and would, someday be potbellied and bandy-legged. But not yet. There was nothing serene about this man. He ran on nervous energy. He was perpetually moving–tapping his foot, whistling under his breath, snapping his fingers, rubbing his eyes, running his hands through his wiry hair. His skin could hardly contain him. He gave the impression that he was too full of life. It came out in extravagant, outrageous laughter and, in his dark moods, depression. At his worst, it erupted in ungovernable rage. Mary Lou had not yet seen his temper. She would, but not yet.

He heard the train pulling in with great snorts and chugs. An ear splitting screech as the brakes were applied announced its arrival. The mammoth beast slid down the track, finally slowing to a stop. A porter descended with a iron footstool. "Watch your step, ma'am."

There she was, tall and straight. Her lustrous dark hair was pulled back from her face. She wore an off white wool dress which skimmed her slender body. Striking as a movie star, she had pinned a small bunch of silk violets at the notch of the collar. He ran toward her, and when she caught sight of him, she laughed and ran to meet him. They were as excited as two children at the county fair.

"I love you."

"I love you."

"Are you sure?"

"Yes, yes, yes, I'm sure, I'm sure."

"Me too. Are we crazy?"

"Yes." And they were, of course.

Don opened the car door for her. His 1931 Ford Roadster was shined to a high gloss for the occasion. He threw her small suitcase into the rumble seat, got behind the wheel and said, "First things first." He kissed her with great gusto. "Oh, Don. Not in public." But she kissed him back.

Don knocked on the door of the white frame house. There was a small sign in the window: Justice of the Peace. A short, balding man of indeterminate age answered the door. He raised his eyebrows in an inquiring look. "Yes?"

"Good afternoon. I'm Don McBride and this is Mary Lou Patterson. We are here to get married."

The man pulled his suspenders up over his shoulders, unrolled his shirt sleeves and buttoned the cuffs. He cleared his throat and nodded. "Well, you've come to the right place. I'll just go get my Bible and a witness." He stepped out of the room, and Don and Mary Lou heard him call, "Ellie Sue, there's a couple out here that look like they can't wait. You'll have to come be a witness." He re-entered the room. His wife, in a wrinkled house dress and fuzzy house shoes, made her appearance. The official looked at Don. "I have to ask you for the three dollars before I do the ceremony."

Don turned to his not-quite-yet bride and said, "Do you have three dollars I can borrow?" It should have been a clue. She rolled her beautiful eyes heavenward, dug around in her purse, and handed him the money.

She whispered to him: "What am I getting into?" Don put her crumpled bills into the outstretched hand of the waiting official. That worthy pocketed his fee, licked his thumb to facilitate the turning of the pages in his Bible, and the ceremony began. It lasted approximately five minutes. In the small space of those minutes, suddenly, now and forevermore, Don and Mary Lou were husband and wife 'til death do them part–Mr. And Mrs. Don Opie McBride. Amen. The honeymoon was nice. Walking back into life in Carnegie was not. Don did not tell her that he had been married and divorced before he was married to Keith. He did not tell her about the son in Kansas. He did not mention the three thousand dollars he owed in debt. There were many important things she did not know. And they went back to Carnegie to face a hostile town.

CARNEGIE–FEBRUARY, 1935

Keith was desperately ill. She had lain in bed since the horrific birth on the nineteenth of January. They packed her with gauze to staunch the bleeding, to no avail. What was a torrent had slowed to a trickle, but the bleeding never stopped. And so she lay, slowly hemorrhaging to death.

They had not brought the baby to her. She believed her child was dead. In her delirium, she sometimes thought she heard a baby cry. She wanted her newborn, but more than that, she wanted to go home to Donald and Carolyn. What would become of them if she couldn't get home? When Don came to visit her, he would reassure her that they were fine. His Aunt Jenny from Nebraska was here helping him take care of them. Keith would smile and nod feebly, and look at him with fever bright eyes, but, in spite of his reassurances, she longed to cuddle her children and tell them how much she loved them. Donald needed his mama. He was five now, and such a big boy. Carolyn was only two. "Oh, dear God, what will happen to my children?" She wept. A nurse came in to take her vital signs. Keith lapsed again into delirium. She lost track of the days. A doctor came from Oklahoma City to administer a transfusion. She had no memory of his coming nor of the procedure.

Then, she seemed to rally a bit. Keith's bleeding had slowed so that the doctor left her room that afternoon feeling guardedly optimistic. It was just after he had left that there was a commotion in the hallway. Someone yelled down the hospital corridor, "There's a house on fire." With the last of her ebbing strength, Keith dragged herself out of bed and to the window. She could see smoke and flames from the west. Her anguished scream added to the confusion. "My babies. Oh, my babies." Nurses ran into the room. They carried her back to her bed and assured her it was not her house that was on fire, but the damage was done. At that moment she felt the blood gush from between her legs as if something had broken in her. Blood soaked through sheets and mattress pad. The nurses moved swiftly to elevate her legs. One hurried out to get the doctor.

They could not get the bleeding under control. Day after weary day passed, and still she bled. Pneumonia set in. It became apparent to everyone that Keith McBride was dying. R.K. and Effie came. Don looked like a ghost walking. Superstitiously, he believed God was punishing him for his many sins. He was responsible for Bernice's pregnancy. He had fathered a child out of wedlock. He never told Keith about them. He had not paid enough attention to Keith. He had been mean to her at times. He had been angry and impatient with her. He had not paid enough attention to Donald and Carolyn. He was angry and harsh with them. He had caused Keith's death. The doctor had told him to be careful, and he impregnated her again. And now, because of it, God was punishing him.

Near the last, he brought the children from home to say good-bye to their mother. Don walked with them to the hospital, and turned the corner into the concrete alley. He carried Carolyn and helped Donald up the long flight of wooden stairs that led to the second floor at the back of the building. Years later, Carolyn would have a vague memory of whitewashed walls and a woman in a bed. Donald remembered it all.

Keith died on March 15 at eleven o'clock in the morning. It had been a long dying.

They took her body home. She lay in a simple casket in the living room where friends and neighbors came to pay their respects. They came and went silently. As they did at all births and deaths, they brought cakes and pies and fried chicken and corn and beans. The food covered the table and the kitchen counter tops, reminiscent of the wedding feast. No one felt like eating. The hush of death fell over the house. A sob, a hug, a murmured word of encouragement broke the silence from time to time.

The adults gathered in the kitchen and drank coffee. Donald and Carolyn crept from behind the bedroom door and looked into the living room, empty except for the casket that held their mother's body. Carolyn pushed a dining room chair up to the casket and struggled to climb up on it. She unwrapped a stick of gum and put it to her mother's mouth.

"No, Carolyn. Get down." Donald pulled at her. "You

can't give mama gum. She's dead. She's gone to heaven to be with Jesus. She can't chew gum anymore." He got her off the chair and pushed it back into place. It was the first time that they were alone together against a hostile world. It would not be the last.

$\mathcal{O}$KLAHOMA CITY–JANUARY, 1993

$\mathcal{C}$arolyn and Don and I sat in the Will Rogers International Airport drinking coffee and waiting for our planes. We had purposely allowed time to debrief. We were all three stunned by our discovery of May Anderson. We all admitted to feeling slightly concussed.

"I have to wonder what life would have been like had Keith lived. I wonder what it would have been like to have had a mother who was affectionate and loving. I never had that, and I've missed it all my life." My brother stirred his coffee.

Carolyn said, "I couldn't believe it when she looked at me and said, 'Honey, I've loved you all of your life.' I wanted to say, 'Where were you when I needed you?' It really makes me ill to think that she was there all that time and we didn't know it."

"I don't remember a baby bed in our home. It makes sense now. You were with the Andersons." My brother shook his head.

"Well, of course. You both would have outgrown the need for a crib. You don't remember a baby bed because there wasn't one there, because I wasn't there."

Carolyn looked at me and said, "I feel sorry for the way you were treated."

Had I been in any condition to take it in, I would have been astonished. Then she added,

"But at least you were loved."

Don took a sip of coffee. "Yes, but look what kind of love it was. It was possessive and controlling and look what was demanded of her in return."

I smiled. "It's going to take me some time to process all of this. I'm just grateful that we found out about our lives."

Don nodded. "The pieces of the puzzle are beginning to fall into place. It's incredible."

Carolyn picked up her camera and stepped over to the side of our table. She snapped our picture. In that snapshot, Don and I are sitting elbow to elbow with our coffee. We both look like owls caught by surprise in bright sunlight–dazed and shocked.

OKLAHOMA CITY–1941-1946

Iced Tea:

No one drank iced tea in the winter. Winter was for drinking Ovaltine. But when the weather changed and became hot enough, people drank iced tea with supper. When the neighborhood children began going barefoot, it was time for iced tea. Everyone looked forward to it.

"Susie, go out there and get me some mint for this tea. (She was the only one who ever called me Susie, using my middle name because she hated my nickname, Bertie.) Two sprigs will do." Mama filled the metal tea ball with black pekoe, screwed on the top and put it in the boiling water.

"Okay, Mama."

On the inside of the kitchen, the sink was in front of the

kitchen window, so whoever was washing dishes could look out at the back yard. The only one who ever "did dishes" back then was mama. On the outside of the house, just under the kitchen window where it was always shady and always cool even on the hottest days, mother grew violets and mint, and in the corner, a huge elephant ear. The hydrant dripped day and night.

In cotton sunsuit and bare feet, I stepped out through the back screen door. It squeaked and then slammed shut with its fifty-times-a-day-when-school-was-out thump. I squatted to pick the mint, tore off a leaf and put it in my mouth. I sucked the juice and spit out the leaf. It tasted exactly like sunshine and summer. I took the two sprigs of mint in to mama. She crushed it and put it in the big glass pitcher from TG&Y. Next came the juice of a fresh lemon and one cup of sugar. Then she added the tea, still hot, which had steeped in the boiling water. I was allowed to stir. We took the ice cube trays from the little freezer compartment in the Frigidaire. The aluminum trays were divided into cubes by a checkerboard of interlocking squares of metal. The cubes were loosened by lifting a metal lever dislodging the ice. We put the ice cubes into tall glasses and poured in the tea. The result was iced tea so sweet and cold it made your teeth sing. It was a sign of summer.

Bob Hope:

Bob Hope came on at nine o'clock. I could stay up long enough to listen to the commercial ("You'll wonder where the yellow went when you brush your teeth with Pepsodent, Pepsodent.") and to hear his introduction: "This is Bob, Fort Bliss, Hope saying, 'I hope, I hope, I hope, I hope, I hope.'" Then I had to go to bed. Bob Hope was funny. Sometimes, though, he told nasty jokes so that organ music would play instead of "The Bob Hope Show." One joke he told was about his lady friend. "I have a girl friend. Her right leg was named "Merry Christmas," and her left leg was named "Happy New Year." She said to me, "Why don't you come up and see me between the holidays." A thousand soldiers and sailors whistled and clapped and stomped, and then organ music came on. Mama said there were laws that would not let bad jokes come on the radio. I didn't get it anyway. Why would anyone name their legs? What a dumb idea.

Jump Rope/Paper Dolls:
We girls jumped rope in the summer time. We would chant in unison:
"Cinderella, dressed in yella, went upstairs to kiss her fella,
How many kisses did she give him? One, two, three.."
until you missed.
Or,
"Shirley Temple went to France,
To teach the ladies how to dance.
How many lessons did she give? One, two, three..."
We jumped "red hot pepper," with two kids turning both ends of the rope as fast as they could. We played hop-scotch. We believed if you stepped on a crack, you would break your mother's back and if you stepped on a hole, you would break your mother's sugar bowl.

On any summer day, little girls would gather to play jacks. They played with a red rubber ball or a golf ball if they were lucky. The jacks were metal–a showering of silver, magenta, blue, and brassy gold. "Onesies" were easy. By the time you got to "tensies" or "elevensies," you had to be good. Summer nights were for "kick the can," or "flashlight." "All-ee, all-ee, out's in free" was the signal that there would be no penalty when you came back in to touch base. Everyone skated on the streets and sidewalks. No one had shoe skates in those days. We all wore Buster Brown oxfords that laced up the front. Skates had leather straps that fit around our ankles. We wore a skate key on a string tied around our necks, and we tightened the clamps to our leather soled shoes.

We would spread a blanket underneath the big oak on our side of the wire fence. Paper dolls occupied our energies for hours on long summer days. Sonja Heine, which we gigglingly pronounced "Heinie," *Gone with the Wind* with all the characters: Clark Gable as Rhett Butler resplendent in his grey morning coat, and Vivien Leigh as Scarlett in her mother's green velvet curtains with the gold fringe. Paper doll clothes had little white paper tabs to hold them on the cardboard doll. The doll cutouts were all dressed in their underwear. It wasn't always easy to keep their clothes on, and if you accidentally cut off a tab, all the other girls screamed and said you had ruined whatever piece of clothing you were cutting out. Scarlett's green velvet dress stayed on her pretty well, but the green velvet hat with the rooster feathers kept falling off her head, because someone had cut off a tab.

When we were tired of paper dolls and jump rope, we collected pop bottles. We would run to Hadley's or Hearth's, the two small family owned grocery stores in our neighborhood, and cash in the bottles for two cents each. When we had cashed in five bottles, we had our dime. It was the price of a cowboy movie at the Tower or the Mayflower. Our mother was often conflicted about allowing us to see movies. Hollywood was the den of iniquity, and she was quite sure that movies were sinful. I doubt that Roy and Dale Rogers, or Gene Autrey led us too far down the path to perdition.

Airfield:

Daddy used to take the Rocket from Oklahoma City to Washington. It was a three day trip, and he always had a Pullman, and he ate his dinner in the dining car. The porter always took good care of daddy, because daddy was generous with tips. Daddy always stayed in the Hay-Adams Hotel in Washington, D. C.

When American Airlines began to take passengers, daddy would fly to Washington. Then, it only took one day. I loved it when he flew. We would go out to the airfield to see him off. All of the lady passengers wore dresses or suits with hats and gloves. The children would be dressed in their Sunday best. Daddy would be dressed in a double breasted business suit, a white dress shirt that my mother had ironed for him, a tie, and shoes shined to mirror gloss. He carried his brief case, a snap open Gladstone brown leather bag. I was so proud of him. He worked for Governor Kerr, and he did important things in our nation's capitol. And when he came home, he brought little salt and pepper shakers he saved from his American Airlines dinner tray.

Dress Up:

Lois Willet took tap. Her mother made her costumes from swishy taffeta, shiny satin, net stiff enough to stand by itself, lots of sequins and diamonds and genuine pearls. I'd never seen anything to beautiful as the pile of fluffy garments thrown across her pink chenille bedspread. My favorite was the red satin number edged in black lace. When we played dress-up, I always grabbed the red satin, and when I put it on, I was transformed before the full length mirror into Carmen Miranda. Carolyn and I did not take tap. Even at our age, we knew that dancing was a sin. All Baptists knew the dangers, and only with the greatest reluctance did our mother allow us to play dress-up with Lois Willet. We wallowed in the illicit pleasure of it.

The Radio:

We pressed our ears to the cathedral-shaped wooden cabinet of the radio. The tall upright was in mama and daddy's bedroom. Mama listened to E.F. Weber every day on WKY. After she had finished her chores and before she had to fix dinner, she sat in the rocking chair in her bedroom with her Bible opened. "God is still on his throne, and prayer changes things," said E. F. Weber. E. F. Weber said it every day, and Mama believed it. But we didn't listen to E. F. Weber. We listened to adventure stories and sent in box tops for the prizes they offered: glow in the dark ray guns and genuine Dick Tracy two way wrist radios. "The William Tell Overture" presaged the adventures of the Lone Ranger and his faithful Indian companion, Tonto. "Hi Ho Silver, away," he shouted to the sound of hoof beats. And then, we heard Tonto say, "Getum up, Scout." In fifteen minutes increments, we heard "Henreeee! Henry Aldrich!" And the adolescent response in a breaking falsetto, "Coming, Mother!" We loved Jack Armstrong, the All American Boy, and, to "The Flight of the Bumblebee," The Green Hornet. We thrilled to Lamont Cranston who had learned "to cloud men's minds so they could not see him." "What evil lurks in the hearts of men? The Shadow knows." This was followed by a spine-chilling, sinister laugh. On Wednesday nights, we walked home from Girls' Auxiliary and Royal Ambassadors. Mama and daddy stayed for prayer meeting. We walked home the twelve city blocks to a darkened and unlocked house. Then, when we were supposed to be getting ready for bed, we would listen to Mr. District Attorney: "And it shall by my duty as District Attorney, not only to prosecute to the limit of the law all persons accused of crimes perpetrated within this county, but to defend with equal vigor the rights and privileges of all its citizens!" Da-ta-ta-DAAAA! Then it was time for "Inner Sanctum," a show so scary it was forbidden to us. Just as the opening sound effects played–the sound of a squeaky door creaking slowly open–the narrator would invite us to come into the inner sanctum, the thought of which was enough to give us nightmares for weeks. At that, we heard daddy's Ford drive up into the driveway, and we ran and jumped into bed and pulled the covers over our heads and pretended to be asleep.

On Saturday nights, everybody in America was glued to their radios to listen to "Your Hit Parade." They played the top ten songs of the week. "Ol' Buttermilk Skies" was number one for so many Saturday nights in a row, I wished it would be something else for a change.

Nancy Drew:

My sister and I were both readers. On long hot summer afternoons we would entertain each other by taking turns reading aloud. The Nancy Drew mystery series was our favorite. This plucky daughter had adventures we could only imagine. She was always getting into and out of impossible scrapes using her unfailing ingenuity: *Nancy Drew and the Spiral Staircase, Nancy Drew and the Old Clock, Nancy Drew at a Dude Ranch.* In one particularly fascinating episode, Nancy Drew had been kidnapped, bound, and gagged by a mad scientist who kept deadly tarantulas in glass jars. As she watched, unable to move and helpless, he unscrewed the lid to one of the jars and the dreadful spider crawled out of the container and crept nearer and nearer to our heroine. The Perils of Pauline could have been no worse. Unhappily, we did not know the word "tarantula," so we sounded it out phonically as we had been taught at Woodrow Wilson Elementary School. All through the story we read with great feeling of the deadly "tare-an-TOO-la." Somehow, something was lost in the translation.

Plastic:

Mama was at the kitchen counter wrapping school lunch sandwiches in waxed paper. Daddy stepped up behind her, wrapped his arms around her, and placed a package in her hands.

"It's a present for you," he said.

She smiled, turned, and opened the box. It was a gaudy red heart on a bright red chain.

"What's it made of?" She turned it over in her hands, fingering the smooth, hard surface..

"It's called plastic," daddy responded. It was indeed, the kind of plastic that, thrown against the wall, would splinter into a million bits and pieces.

"What's it for?" she asked. "What are they going to make out of it?"

Daddy took the necklace and hung it around her neck. I thought it was beautiful–a symbol of my daddy's love. "Women's jewelry, I think," he responded. "It's new stuff."

$\mathcal{K}$NOXVILLE–1977

$\mathcal{W}$hen she got the phone call from daddy that mother was dying, Carolyn threw some clothes in a bag, brewed a thermos of coffee, and immediately set out to drive from Fort Wayne to Knoxville. She started her trip at ten o'clock at night. It was in the days when CB radios were the rage. She had one, of course. Her handle was "Chigger." When she began to feel drowsy, she got on her CB and talked to the truckers.

"This is Chigger and this is a distress call. Is anyone out there? My mother is dying, and I have to get to Knoxville and I'm driving alone. I am trying to stay awake. This is Chigger. Please come in." Two truckers answered her call.

"Okay, Chigger. I'm going your way. My handle is Daddy-O. Follow me and I'll talk you in. Ten-four."

"Chigger, this is Big Dog. You follow Daddy-O and I'll follow you. You are not alone. We'll get you there. Ten-four."

All that long night, she drove between those two huge trucks. The three of them talked through the darkness. When they got to Knoxville, she took the West Hills exit.

"Thanks, guys. I appreciate your help. This is Chigger signing off. Ten-four."

The two truckers saluted her with a toot of their air horns. There are some good and gallant men out there on the highways–latter day knights in shining armor ready to help a damsel in distress. It was dawn when she drove into the driveway of the house on Chesterfield Drive. Safe home.

Mother sat up in bed and clutched at my arm. "Did you know my mother died? I'm so distressed. I'm so distressed." She lapsed back into half consciousness.

"Yes. I know. You're all right." I looked up at daddy. "How old was she when her mother died–eighteen?"

"I think that's right. She's back in time. She's a girl again. Go get a cup of coffee. I'll stay with her."

I walked into the kitchen where Don and Carolyn were drinking coffee and poured myself a cup. "Carolyn, she's asking for you. Go in there, and get daddy to come out for awhile. He can't take much more of this." I sat across the formica topped maple table. Deep lines of exhaustion marked my brother's face. "We've got to get some sleep. She's back somewhere in time. She's talking about her mother's death."

My brother nodded agreement. "I know she wants to die at home, but the hospice nurse told us if we changed our minds, we could call and they'd get her to the hospital. What do you think?"

"I say we honor her wishes. I'm okay. At least there are four of us."

"Was she really calling for Carolyn?"

"No. I told her that because Carolyn needs to believe it. When I got here yesterday, Carolyn told me she was leaving. She said, 'Now that you're here, mother won't want me anymore, and I'm the one who has been cleaning up her crap for a week.' I begged her to stay. I think if you have spent most of your life hating someone and spent a year or so trying to make it right, when death comes, you are in some kind of emotional turmoil."

Donald nodded. "Carolyn is pretty high strung. She's been in emotional turmoil most of her life."

"You think so?" Our laughter had a touch of hysteria. We were all naturally wound tight. And we were all looney from lack of sleep and emotional distress. "Maybe we're all a little crazy."

TELLICO PLAINS, TENNESSEE–1925

Mary Lou felt small and lost. Everyone was in shock. How could her mother have died? Her mother, Grace, had borne nine children and buried three–three little boys named Frank,

Virgil, and Howard. And now, she and the newest baby would join them in the churchyard cemetery. The thoughts raced through Mary Lou's head. Mother is gone. She is with her children in heaven. But what about her children on earth? Dear God. What would they do now? Mary Lou was the oldest girl. She had always helped with her younger brothers and sisters. What would dad do, now? She would have to be strong for her dad. Paul was only five and Ann eight. She put the flat iron back on the wood stove to heat and picked up the other iron. She spit on her finger and barely touched it to the iron's flat surface to test the heat. It sizzled. She finished the shirt with the last few strokes and hung it up. Her dad would wear it to the funeral.

Mary Lou helped get the little kids ready. She wet Paul's hair and slicked it back. She brushed Ann's hair and helped get her shoes laced. The two littlest ones didn't seem to know what was happening. Their mother and the new baby were laid out in the parlor. Last night friends and neighbors came in to sit up. Only the children slept. The adults sat up all night, talked, drank coffee, and comforted each other. Mary Lou's emotions ranged from sorrow to panic. She felt she couldn't breathe and that she would die, too. Too soon, it was time to begin the sad journey to the church at Sink. Six men carried the casket out the parlor door and loaded it onto a wagon. The family followed in a second wagon. The trip to the church took an hour. They arrived and found that folks were gathering. Mary Lou averted her gaze as they passed the cemetery where the newly dug grave stood out, shocking and garishly red, from the surrounding green. The family filed in. The small sanctuary was filled with mourners who had come to pay their respects. At Beulah Methodist Church, the custom was to have an open casket. People filed by to see the bodies of Grace Patterson and her newborn child. Mary Lou thought she could not bear the crushing weight of her loss.

It was time for the service to begin. The congregation stood to sing "Gathering Buds."

"Jesus has taken a beautiful bud out of our garden of love.

Borne it away to the city of God, home of the angels above.

Gathering buds, gathering buds, wonderful care will be given,

Jesus is gathering, day after day, buds for the palace of heaven.

Father and mothers, weep not or be sad, still on the Savior rely;

You shall behold them again and be glad, beautiful flowers on high."

Grief and sorrow dogged her weary steps as she followed the crowd of neighbors and friends from the church to the freshly dug grave. Ann's eyes were red from crying. Paul looked lost. What must be going on inside his head. Mary Lou put her arm around her littlest brother. "It's going to be all right, Paul. I'll take care of you."

"I want my Mama."

"Oh, honey, I want her, too."

Paul watched as they lowered the casket into the red earth of the open grave. "Why are they putting my Mama in a hole in the ground?" He wanted to rush at them and make them stop. Mary Lou held him fast in her grasp.

Mary Lou quit her teaching job and stayed home after her mother died. She cared for her younger siblings, and she worked in her dad's store. She cooked for the family and kept their clothes clean and in order. It was not until after Grand-daddy Patterson married Mrs. Ferguson that Mary Lou decided to go to Howard Henderson Hospital in Knoxville to do her nurse's training. Mary Lou gave her dad six years of her life in order to keep the family together. Granddaddy always said, "As long as I have a dollar, fifty cents of it belongs to Mary Lou."

RICHMOND–2001

My Uncle Paul and I talk on the phone fairly often. Inevitably, we speak of our shared love for Mary Lou. She had not been a biological mother to either of us, but had been a true mother to us both. I asked him what he remembered about Grace—his mother who had died in childbirth when he was five. He told me of a recurring dream that has come to him over the years even into his eighth decade. "I dream that I am at Beulah cemetery. I look up and I see my mother in the doorway of the church. She is more beautiful than anything I have ever seen on earth. In my dream, I run toward her. She smiles and holds out her arms to me. And when I get to the church door, she vanishes. I have dreamed that dream all my life."

Do we look for our mother all our lives? Do we wish for her vitality and beauty and selflessness? Do we seek her in our friendships, in our lovers, in our marriages? Do we continue to want the kind of nurturing love that we knew as infants, when our slightest distress was quickly soothed by loving hands. Or, if our mothers were dead, or absent, or incompetent, or distant, do we still frantically seek the love we desperately need and never received? Are we doomed to live, forever and always, hoping the next relationship will meet our every need? As a flower turns its face to the warmth of the sun, we seek the life-giver.

CHORES-1945

Mother slopped her rag into the gray water of the galvanized bucket, rinsed it (she would have said "rinched"), flapped it once and sprinkled on Old Dutch Cleanser. She moved along the periphery of the kitchen linoleum on hands and knees, washing the baseboard that encircled the room. Her mournful soprano accompanied her chore.

"Tempted and tried, we're oft made to wonder
Why it should be thus all the day long,
While there are others living about us,
Never molested, though in the wrong.
Farther along, we'll know all about it.
Farther along, we'll understand why.
Cheer up, my brother. Walk in the sunshine.
We'll understand it all bye and bye."

The house was her world, her prison: the kitchen, her domain. Her mother-in-law, my grandmother, my daddy's mother, said, "I'll go up against anyone in the kitchen except Mary Lou."

In truth, she was a superb cook of the pinch of this and handful of that variety. Butterhorn rolls were a specialty. On Sundays, they replaced the daily biscuits and cornbread. It was a miracle to watch her roll out the yeasty dough into a perfect circle, cut pie slice triangles, dip a slice into melted butter, roll it up beginning with the blunt end, dip that into sesame seed and place it in the row on a shallow pan to rise.

Sunday smelled different from any other day. She got up early to "put on" a roast. It would be done by the time church was over—juicy on the inside and crisp on the outside. The Fullers and the Moseleys and the Whites often came to our house for Sunday dinner with all their kids. The women would spread the dining room table with mother's best damask table cloth, freshly ironed and smelling of clean air and sunshine. They would get out the china and Lady Hamilton silver plate. When it was time to eat, the grownups ate at the big table, and all the children ate around the table in the breakfast nook—roast beef, gravy made from drippings, mashed potatoes made with Pet milk or Carnation, green beans (Kentucky wonders from our garden), squash casserole, Jell-O salad with mayonnaise and a cherry on top, the butterhorn rolls with real butter and her peach conserve.

The garbage man once told her that she had the cleanest garbage he had ever seen. He said he could tell what kind of a housekeeper someone was by looking at their garbage. That made her very proud. It also made her more careful about the way she disposed of refuse.

My mother had married my daddy, a widower with three children. He had loudly proclaimed, "No wife of mine is going to work." It was almost impossible for me to believe she was ever anything other than my mother.

She was put on this earth to wash clothes every Monday in a wringer washing machine with separate tubs of rinse water and blueing and a pan of hot Faultless starch. Clothes were separated into piles—delicate, white, colored, heavy. Delicates were washed by hand. Whites went into the washing machine first, dipped from the tub with a big wooden spoon, put through the wringer into the rinse water. They were run through the wringer a second time and into the tub with blueing and then passed through the wringer again. This was repeated for each pile of clothes. As the clothes came out of that process, they were placed into a bushel basket, carried to the back yard, hung on the clothesline—a thick, smooth, blueish-black wire attached to a tree on one side and a pole on the other, supported in the middle by another pole. Each piece of clothing was held in place by wooden pins–prewar ones had a metal hinge. The more recent ones were simply made from wood and were not nearly as good as the old ones. As the clothes dried, they were brought into the kitchen and sprinkled down. Mama used a pop bottle with a hole made by a nail in the lid. Every piece of laundry was sprinkled, wadded, and pushed down into the bushel basket.

Everything was ironed on Tuesday, including sheets and starched pillow cases, and daddy's white shirts. Everything was made of one hundred percent cotton or linen. Tuesday was ironing day. Mama hated Tuesday. She stood at the ironing board all the long day. At noon, the radio station began broadcasting the soap operas: "Helen Trent," "Lorenzo Jones and His Wife, Belle," "Ma Perkins." For fifteen minutes, each drama would unfold at an excruciatingly slow pace. The dialogue was standard:

"John, I don't know how to tell you."

"Tell me what, Doris?"

"I just can't say it." (Female sobbing to rising minor chords from the organ.)

"Please, Doris. You must get hold of yourself and tell me."

The announcer would come on and tell us to tune in tomorrow to see if Doris would finally tell John whatever it was she needed to tell him. Then there would be a commercial: "Rinso white, Rinso Bright, Happy little washday song." Or, "Ivory soap, ninety nine and ninety nine one hundreths per cent pure. It floats." Then it was time to cook dinner. "No wife of mine is going to work," said Daddy. Mostly, he worked in an office. She was just a housewife.

She was put on earth to grow and cook and can our

food—great quantities of beans and corn, peaches and pickles, sauerkraut she fermented in a great stone crock on the back porch, chow-chow, and chili sauce made from bushels of ripe tomatoes. She poured boiling water over them and slipped the skins off and cooked them on the stove in an oval cast iron pot she had simmering with onions and green bell peppers and sugar.

She was born to garden—to grow our vegetables: asparagus and eggplant and squash and always beans and tomatoes. Everything she touched grew for her: roses—Blaze, Radiance, and Bishop Darlington. She grew marigolds and zinnias, clematis and hydrangeas. By the time I was in first grade, I knew them all by name: pansies, snapdragons, larkspur and daisies, tulips and iris, hyacinths, dahlias and gladiola, lilac and wisteria and chrysanthemum in the fall. I couldn't imagine that she had ever been anything before she was my mother. But she was.

Tellico Plains, Tennessee—1910

From the time she was old enough to stand on a kitchen chair, she made biscuits and cornbread for large crowds of people. She did it every day. Her mother cooked dinner for the threshing hands that worked the farm. Mary Lou made the bread. She had one older brother, but she was the oldest girl. As long as she could remember, there was always a baby in the house. Children on a Tennessee farm in 1910 were considered assets. They worked. No one entertained them. It did not occur to them to be bored. They made their own fun, but only after they had done their work. My mother grew up helping her mother cook, clean, and take care of small children. When the brothers and sisters found time for play, they invented their own. The girls would build houses from autumn leaves. They would live within the circle of imaginary walls. The boys would be bears and growl outside the girls' playhouse. Children were kept innocent and uninformed about adult matters. Mary Lou was late going into puberty. She began her periods at sixteen and had no idea what had happened to her. She went to her mother.

"I think there's something wrong with me. There is blood on my clothes."

"Put your things on that chair. I'll wash them for you." There was no word of explanation. My grandmother was too embarrassed to discuss the matter with her daughter. A few days later, her mother sent Mary Lou to an old granny who served as a local midwife. My mother learned about menstruation from the old woman. It was not a subject that would ever be discussed between mother and daughter.

*S*INK–1923

*M*ary Lou looked up at the darkening sky with some misgivings. She had decided to risk it. Because she really wanted to go home for the weekend, she had dismissed her class of children early because of the coming storm. Her one room school house was clean and straight and ready for next week. At seventeen, she was hardly old enough to be teaching these mountain children. The big boys, whom she hoped would stay in school and finish the sixth grade, had helped her move some boxes that morning. Her other students were three first graders, two sixth graders, and ten children second through fifth grades. She boarded with a family during the week, but now, she wanted to get home to her mother. Teaching school was something she loved, but she didn't know if she would teach again next year.

The air was oppressive. It had a metallic odor. The mule she rode was skittish with the first raindrops. She dug in her heels and he plodded along. Then it hit. Lightening flashed across the blackening sky. Thunder clapped and echoed through the hills, the crashing sound careened crazily down the mountainside and through the valleys. The rain fell in torrents. She was instantly soaked to the skin and felt fear prickle at the back of her neck to run down her arms to her fingertips. She urged her mule on. He stumbled in the red slop of the road. Lightening struck, and a pine tree snapped and crashed to the ground. As they came to the creek, she could hear the sound of rushing waters, but she could not turn back now. Her mule balked at the edge of the torrent. She breathed a quick prayer and urged him into the rushing waters. The creek was swollen beyond recognition. Where was all this water coming from? She was in the middle of it now, and water rose until it covered her legs. The mule snorted in fear, but did not stop. He lost his footing, stumbled, and fell into the rushing stream. Mary Lou held on with all her strength. With one mighty effort, the animal gained his footing and carried her at last to safety on the other side. Just around the next bend, she could see the house. With enormous relief, she urged the tired mule onward. Soon she caught sight of the house. As she approached, she saw her mother, dish towel in hand, standing on the porch watching for her. Mary Lou dismounted and ran the last few steps toward home, leaving the tired mule to be tended by her brother. Her mother's relief was palpable. She stood with open, welcoming arms. "Oh, honey," she said. "I knew you'd come." And together they went in to the warmth of the kitchen.

$\mathcal{C}$URITIBA, PARANA, BRAZIL–1974

$\mathcal{O}$ur children attended the International School of Curitiba, first through eighth grades. My husband, Bill, was the president of its board. The faculty was a mixture of North Americans: former missionary kids, now grown, who had gone back to the States and received their degrees in education and come back home to Brazil to live their adult lives; Canadian teachers who enjoyed living overseas; missionaries who volunteered to take some time from their own busy schedules to drop in once a week and teach art or music. The school had eight grades. The student body was eclectic– American missionary kids, German children whose parents were in Brazil with German companies, the children of diplomats, Brazilian youngsters whose parents wanted them to learn English. The English-speaking community was served by the school.

Before our son, Mark, completed eighth grade, we began to think of his high school education. We thought, perhaps, he would be going to high school in Amarillo where his Damon relatives lived. When the time came, things didn't work out that way. I began to feel anxious. I wrote to my parents explaining what our situation was. In reply, I received a letter from my father. It was dated November 13, 1974.

"Dear Bertie,

I am going to exercise the prerogative of a father to his daughter. I am fully aware of your anxiety over an offspring, but you need to slow down a bit and exercise some faith and stop worrying over Mark's situation. Honey, we will look into the problem of Mark's attending Chilhowee Academy, and if it works out, and I hope it does, we will be very pleased to have Mark with us at holiday and weekends, and will look after his needs such as clothes, books, and other things. I've got enough faith in Mark to know he will make it just fine. And we love him.

Before the Chilhowee situation surfaced, your mother had made up her mind that Mark could stay with us and go to school here, but although that would be all right, I am concerned about her health. I asked her to talk to her doctor before making up our minds. She said that would be silly. Anyway, the Lord is and will work this out so quit chewing your nails and thank Him for looking after you and yours. Max Hardin in our church and Mary went to Chilhowee and we will talk to him before I go over to the school. But we will get all the information, find out about fees and so on.

Honey, your dad loves you very, very much and your problems are ours.

Dad"

What a relief! As it turned out, the gritty reality was more difficult for my father to deal with than the vision he had of it when he wrote the letter. Mark did go to Chilhowee for his junior year. He was fifteen years old. We put him on a plane by himself. It was like dying to see our child board that plane alone. Mark went to Knoxville. Daddy met him at the airport and took him home. The next day, he was enrolled in Harrison Chilhowee Baptist Academy, run by the Baptists of Tennessee. The next summer, the rest of the family came to the States for a year's furlough. It was good to be home. A year seems a long time when you are anticipating it. When it's over, it seems like no time at all.

KNOXVILLE-1977

We had come to the States on a year's furlough in time to celebrate bicentennial of our country. Now, it was time for us to go back to Brazil and to our work. Had we really been in the States for a year? It seemed like yesterday that daddy had met us at the airport. "Honey," he had said. "You won't have your mother for this whole year. The doctor says she can't possibly live that long." I remembered the sharp pain of the thought. But I had responded, "Daddy, I've asked the Lord for this year with her and I know He is going to grant my request." And He did.

It had been a wonderful year. We lived for the twelve months on the campus of Harrison Chilhowee Academy in Seymour, where Mark and Paul were in school. Every morning I would get the boys off to school, give the house a lick and a promise, and go into Knoxville to spend the day with my mother. She was homebound with a heart condition. She had asked me to teach her Sunday School class of young married women at West Hills Baptist Church for the year I was home. I told her I would if she would help me prepare the lessons. Every day we sat on her sofa in the den and studied the Bible. And we talked and laughed and cried together. She told me things she had never told me—of the man she almost married instead of daddy; of his son, Tommy; of being a nurse to Keith while she was dying in the Carnegie hospital; of taking care of Carolyn and Donald before she married daddy; of seeing daddy come in and pick up the laundry at the hospital and not giving him a second glance. Then, one day, she told me about the night I was born.

Mary Lou set her coffee cup on the end table beside the tweed-covered couch. She sat on one end of the sofa, tucked her legs under her, and pulled the afghan over her knees. I sat on the other end of the couch, curled up, facing her. She began her story.

"I was living at Ray's house on the farm a few miles from Carnegie. I woke up in the middle of the night and there was a light in my room. I knew it was the presence of the Lord. I did not hear a voice, but the Presence was real. I sat on the side of my bed and waited, and then the light was gone. I tried to go back to sleep and couldn't. I pondered what it might be. I got up and looked out of the window to see if there was a light anywhere, but it was dark as only it can be out in the country at night. I finally went back to sleep. About an hour later, there was a knock at the door. Someone had come to say there was a woman in difficult labor and I was to get to the hospital. So I got dressed and went to the hospital in time to help with your delivery. I gave you your first bath. Then, of course, later your mother died, and then after that, I married your daddy and you were really my child. I have loved you from the moment you were born. I just didn't know I would get to keep you." She paused and shook her head. "There was the light in my room that night. It's a great mystery to me–a great mystery."

Now it was time to go back to our work. Daddy said it was time to get to the airport. There was a flurry of activity as the men loaded the car with our luggage. Mama was too sick to go. I went back to her bedroom to say my goodbyes. I thought I could not bear it. The pain of parting burned in my chest and throat and the tears rose from my heart and gathered in my eyes. She was standing shakily. I knew that I might not see her again on this earth. She looked at me as if she were memorizing my face. In a stricken voice she said to me, "When I was seventeen, I rode an old mule from Sink up to home in a terrible storm. When I got there, my mother was watching and waiting for me. She said, 'Oh, honey, I knew you'd come.' Don't you worry about me. I've weathered many a storm and I'll get through this one. When I get to heaven, my mama will be waiting for me and she'll say those words to me again: 'Oh honey, I knew you'd come.'"

"I know, Mama. I know. I do love you so much."

"I love you, honey."

And we stood for a moment, heart to broken heart.

KNOXVILLE–1984

Years after my parents' death, I drove from Richmond to Fort Worth to defend my dissertation. I seldom had an occasion to go to Knoxville, but, that time, I drove through the city and made my accustomed stops. I drove by Chesterfield Drive and stopped at the house my parents had lived in the last years of their lives. Someone else lived there now. I sat for long moments looking at the trees and shrubs my father had planted so long ago. I allowed the memories to well up as I sat and stared. My parents had been gardeners of the first order. The yards of all the houses they had occupied were always meticulously kept. In the spring, people would drive by to see their flowers. Daddy used to say, "My wife is the one with the green thumb. I'm the one with the strong back." I looked at this yard where my father had spent so many hours mowing, mulching, planting, pruning. Now, the old place looked shabby. It was time to move on.

I drove to the nearest florist and bought roses. They were beautiful, as all roses are beautiful. These were almost as beautiful as the ones daddy had cultivated. I turned onto Kingston Pike and drove to the memorial gardens. I drove slowly through the cemetery, up to the crest of the hill. I put the flowers on their graves, with a prayer. I did not linger. As I left, I looked back once. The view from their resting place is magnificent. I have no sense of their presence in this place.

I decided to drive down Kingston Pike and visit the old building that was Howard Henderson Hospital so many years ago. Kingston Pike is now crowded with banks, shops, restaurants, and other commercial entities. I was headed toward downtown. The traffic was, as usual, noisy and congested. I looked up the hill to my left and caught sight of the old building. I managed to make a left turn onto the property, drive up the long driveway, and park near the front. The building looks strangely out of place now, like a southern belle in graceful skirts and lace shawl at a hoedown. It is, of course, columned. Tall, floor to ceiling windows stand behind the columns. The wavering images of the window's glass attest to its age. The porch is deep. Its shade invites the traveler. My mother told me once that when she was there as a student, and then as a nurse in the 1930s, there was nothing between the hospital and the river but rolling, lushly green, well-tended lawns. I climbed the broad steps leading to the porch and stepped inside the foyer. I needed a moment for my eyes to adjust from the glare of the afternoon sun to the dim interior. I stood in a circular rotunda and looked up at the high ceiling and the ornate chandelier, amazed to find black and white tiles on the floor and a tall, curved, mahogany counter that surely had served as the admissions desk for the hospital. I was certain that both features were original to the structure. I looked to my right and realized that there was now a beauty salon in what must have been a day room years ago. I walked in and asked to speak to the owner. A young man with a pony tail and a gold earring looked at me. "I'm the owner." He was slathering mousse on the hair of a customer.

I introduced myself. "Do you mind telling me how long you have owned this building?"

"Well, let's see. We moved in here September a year ago."

"Did you know that this building was originally a hospital?"

"Someone said that it was. That must have been a long time ago."

"Yes. Yes, it was. It was a very long time ago."

KNOXVILLE–1933

After a mine disaster in Alabama, the casualties were taken by train as far north as Knoxville. A dying man was brought to Howard Henderson Hospital where my mother was on night duty. She had graduated the year before. Looking very professional, she was dressed in her crisp, white cotton uniform and her starched nurse's cap pinned to her dark bobbed hair. She wore black cotton stockings and sensible shoes. At twenty-eight years old, she had already done enough living for three lifetimes. She sat at the dimly lit nurses station in the beautiful old hospital on the hill, completing her charts in her neat handwriting, and meticulously logging the vital information. The call light went on, signaling her that she was needed in the room of the injured patient. Her uniform whispered in the silence as she strode down the deserted hallway with her rubber-soled shoes making no sound on the glossy linoleum. She approached the bed of the patient. He was conscious and writhing in pain. As she reached to brush his disheveled hair from his brow, he grabbed her wrist.

"Help me, lady, help me," he rasped. "I'm dying and I'm going to hell."

Shocked at the strength of his grasp, and at the desperation in his voice, she sought to comfort him.

"You are going to be all right." She felt inadequate before his blazing eyes. For a fleeting moment, she felt as though she were looking into the mouth of hell itself.

"Tell me how to be saved, Lady. Don't let me die this way. Please."

She was a Christian, but she had never been faced with a situation like this. Certainly, she had never told anyone how to die in hope. She stumbled through an explanation of how Jesus had died so that anyone who believes might have eternal life.

"Yes," he said. "Yes. I believe. I'm safe."

Later that night, he died, leaving her shaken and awed.

Dr. Howard was a kind old gentleman. Dr. Henderson was a terror. He abused the nurses and cursed through surgery. One early morning, a patient was rolled into the operating room. Dr. Henderson, scrubbed and irritable, came in prepared to perform surgery. He took one look at the instruments laid out on the table and thundered, "Damn you! Those are the wrong instruments."

Mary Lou stiffened her back and in a voice that could freeze hell replied, "Dr. Henderson, those are the instruments you requested, and you will not talk to me that way or you will be doing this surgery without the benefit of an attending nurse."

He glanced at her, saw that she meant it, gave a brief nod, winked, and said, "Attagirl."

A mountain man was a patient at Howard-Henderson. He was there for many months. In the process of his healing, he was administered morphine for pain, and he became addicted. Mary Lou went in to talk to Dr. Howard.

"Dr. Howard, I need to talk to you about Mr. Snydor."

"Yes, Miss Patterson?"

"He's addicted to morphine."

"I know."

"I wonder if you would give me permission to get him off the drug."

"How do you intend to do that, Miss Patterson?"

"If you would let me cut the dosage just a bit every day, I think I might be able to do it."

Dr. Howard stretched and yawned. "Yes. That's okay. I'll write you an order."

"Thank you, doctor. And would you write a prescription for sugar pills while you're at it?"

He looked up from under bushy brows. "You don't ask much. Yes. I'll do it."

She smiled and went back to the nurses' station. Every day the little scene played itself out:

"Good morning, Mr. Snydor. I have your morphine for you. And these are very strong pills Dr. Howard has ordered for you. They will cut the pain. He said that you only need one, but I've asked if I can give you two."

"Thank you kindly, Miss Mary Lou. You're a good girl. You're good to me. You make me feel better just coming in to my room."

And, "How are you feeling today, Mr. Snydor? Here are your pills. Let's turn you over so I can give you this morphine."

"I'm feeling some better. I think it's those pills that are helping me."

Every day the amount of morphine decreased. Every day the amount of sterile water in the syringe increased. Little by little by little.

Finally, she was giving injections of sterile water and one half of a sugar pill. Then, the day came when he was to be released from the hospital. All the staff gathered around to say goodbye to Mr. Snydor. He was drug free, clean, and well.

One of the doctors said to him, "Mr. Snydor, is there anything here you would like to take home with you?"

Mr. Snydor grinned.

"Reckon so."

"What would you like to take home with you?"

He pointed directly at Mary Lou.

"Her."

Vonore, Tennessee–1994

Of course, by that time your mother was married to Dewey Hooper." My Uncle Paul shifted in his recliner. We had been talking about the death of his mother when he was five, and about the fact that my mother, his sister, was eighteen at the time and she took over mothering her younger siblings.

"What? What did you say? Did you say my mother was married before she married daddy?"

"You didn't know that?"

"No! Are you sure? Was she a bigamist?"

"Oh no. There was a divorce."

"Are you sure about that?" I was gasping in astonishment. "She was divorced? What year was that? Were there any children?"

"No, there was no child. She wasn't married very long. Let's see. The divorce was in the early part of the depression—1929 or 1930."

"My mother was divorced! Ann, did you know about this?"

"Sure, I knew." My aunt looked extremely uncomfortable.

"Why did they divorce?"

"He was not good to her."

"Do you mean he was abusive? Why didn't someone tell me? I'm an adult. I can take it." My aunt crossed her arms and cleared her throat. "I have a picture of him somewhere. He was just a local man there in Tellico. I remember once when your mother and I were back visiting Dad for the summer. We saw Dewey Hooper down at the garage. He was working on a car. He didn't see us and we didn't speak."

"Did daddy know?"

"No, never. Mary Lou didn't want him to know, and I never told."

"What's wrong with this family? Why all the secrecy?"

Later, Ann sent me the snapshot of mother when she was married to Dewey Hooper. Granddaddy Patterson, Mary Lou, Paul, and Dewey Hooper are standing on a flight of steps. Granddaddy looks like he always did. He is standing on a step above the others. Mary Lou is wearing a long coat with a fur collar, black stockings, and a slightly sour expression. Uncle Paul is about ten years old in the picture. He has on a light colored double breasted suit and a pork- pie hat and looks the picture of fashion. He is standing between Mary Lou and her husband. Dewey Hooper is slouching. His hat is on the back of his head, his hands are in his pockets, and a cigarette is dangling from his mouth. Sneering, he looks insolent—or maybe defensive. Dewy Hooper could have been elected the poster child for ne'er-do-wells.

Several weeks after my conversation with Uncle Paul, a thick envelope arrived at home addressed to me. My Uncle Paul was a mail carrier for many years, but he never writes a letter. I was surprised to see the return address. Paul had obtained, from the Knox County archives, a copy of the divorce decree dissolving the marriage between my mother and Dewey Hooper. I opened it with trembling fingers. In legalese, I read that Dewey Hooper didn't show up in court and that he "has wholly failed, refused and neglected to provide for and support the complainant, Mary Lou Hooper. The Court further finds and so adjudges and decrees that the defendant willfully, maliciously, and unlawfully deserted and abandoned the complainant in November, 1928, without any cause of just excuse, and that his said desertion and abandonment of her has been continuous ever since. The Court finds and so adjudges and decrees that the complainant, Mary Lou Hooper, has been true to her marriage vows and has given the defendant, Dewey Hooper, no cause or just excuse for his said misconduct, nor has she condoned the same." The decree went on to "hereby forever and perpetually" dissolve the marriage, declared the complainant an unmarried woman, and her maiden name, Mary Lou Patterson was restored to her. I had to laugh at the last paragraph. "The costs of this cause are adjudged against the defendant, Dewey Hooper, the eleven dollars heretofore paid into Court by the complainant, Mary Lou Hooper, shall by the Clerk be applied upon said costs, and in case the costs are made out of the defendant, then the eleven dollars heretofore paid into Court by the complainant shall be returned to her." It was entered September 30, 1930, and signed by Hu B. Webster, Judge. My mother was a twenty-three-year-old divorced woman in 1930! It was hard for me to absorb the information. I wondered if she ever got her eleven dollars back. I looked at the date again. Five years and five days later, my mother married our dad. And if my memory served me correctly, they used to tell how he had to borrow the three dollars from her for their wedding license. Dadgum, they get you coming and going.

BRAZIL-KNOXVILLE—1975

We were not due a furlough until 1976–the bicentennial year. We had a year to go before we could go to the States. My mother had been diagnosed with a heart condition. During all of 1975, she was in and out of the hospital. We had been in Brazil nine years by then. Daddy called and asked if I might be able to come to Knoxville for a month. He said he thought my presence might be the kind of medicine mama needed. I had not seen my mother for four years at that time. In those years, it was the policy of our sending agency not to allow those kinds of trips, but our area director, Dr. Frank Means, gave me permission to go at my own expense.

I was traveling alone. I was to fly from Curitiba to Rio to New York to Knoxville. We usually went through Miami, but the best ticketing took me through New York that time. I had heard terrible things about how rude New Yorkers were. I was dreading having to deal with any one of them. I knew I would be fine. I had no fear about being alone. After all, I spoke the language, but I didn't like the idea of New York.

Nine hours after leaving Rio on a night flight, we were coming into New York City. Sleepy travelers lined up to use the lavatories. I brushed my hair, arranged my wrinkled clothes, and put on my shoes. I steeled myself for La Guardia.

I soon found myself in line, holding tightly to my passport. One by one, my fellow passengers stepped up to the official to present their passports. I stood behind the yellow line, waiting. When it was my turn, I stepped up and handed my passport to the waiting agent. The man took it, glanced at it, thumbed through it, and must have noticed I had been out of the country for four years. He looked up, smiled broadly at me, and with twinkling eyes, he tenderly said, "Welcome home, Roberta." I teared, choked, swallowed hard, and nodded my thanks. New York was wonderful! I was on my way to Knoxville. I was on my way to see my mother. I was on my way home.

$\mathcal{K}$NOXVILLE—1975

$\mathcal{O}$ur reunion was warm, wonderful, and healing. Inevitably, my time at home flew by, and it was time to say good-bye again. My dad took me to the Knoxville airport. He hugged me, thrust an envelope into my hands, and said, "Don't read this until you're on the plane." And then, he was gone. I didn't wait until I was on the plane. As soon as I found a place to wait for boarding, I opened it. He wrote:

"Bertie,
Sometimes words don't come out right. Even prayers are not what the heart wants to say. How can I tell you how much I love you? How can you know what I wish I could say? There is a chance that one or both of us will be in heaven when you come back in 1976. I thank God that one day we will be at home together forever. Don't grieve for us. I thank God for what we have had, and what we will experience. Do you remember I wrote a little poem once:

I dare not look at the hour glass.
Noontime came. I saw it pass.
The shadows now grow slim and tall.
Sunset writes upon the wall.
I seem to hear the grains slip through
And I know the sands of time are few.
If you cry, cry tears of joy because we will not be separated.
Your Dad"

I suddenly remembered the moment just before daddy walked me down the aisle at my wedding so many years before. I looked at him through my veil and said, "I love you, Daddy." He had said, "I love you, too, honey." Someone said that if the world were coming to an end, and we all had ten minutes warning, all of the phone lines around the globe would be clogged with people stammering out the words, "I love you." What else is there to say?

OKLAHOMA CITY—1976

I was asked to speak in the general assembly of an adult Sunday School department in Northwest Baptist Church as a part of furlough deputation. I spoke of our work in Brazil and the responsiveness and warmth of the people in the land of the Southern Cross. After my presentation, a woman came up to me and said, "My name is Wanda Cinnamon—just like the spice. Your mother was my Sunday School teacher in Trinity Baptist Church here in Oklahoma City during World War II. My husband was overseas. He was serving in Italy. I remember that your mother came to my house to visit me one morning after I had been to her class the Sunday before.

She came in. I remember the housecoat I was wearing. She asked me if I were a Christian and when I told her I was not, she asked if she could share with me how to accept Christ. She opened her Bible and showed me verses that told me how God loves me. We knelt to pray in front of my sofa. I wept as I prayed and my tears stained the sofa. Those stains stayed on that sofa as long as I had it. I could never wash them out. I wrote to my husband and told him what had happened to me. I told him to talk to a chaplain. My husband accepted Christ in Italy and was baptized in the ocean by an Army chaplain. After the war, he came home safe to me. Tell your mother that all of our children are Christians. Tell her because of her, we all know the Lord."

Her story moved me deeply. When I could regain my composure enough to speak, all I could say was, "Thank you, thank you for sharing that. She'll be so happy to hear that I've met you. She'll be so happy to hear about your family. She is not well. This will bring her such joy."

Curitiba–November 1977

Daddy called our house. The connection between the States and Brazil was often full of static, but he came in clearly. "Honey, if you want to see your mother again, you'd better come on home."

I felt the weight of dread in my chest. "Daddy, there is no way I can get out of here. It takes two weeks to get police clearance." My voice shook with distress.

My husband took the phone from my hand. "Don, send us a telegram as soon as we hang up. I'll need it to get her out of Brazil. Just say that her mom is dying. Do it now. I'll have

Roberta in Knoxville by tomorrow night." And he hung up the receiver.

"Go pack a bag." I looked at him as if he'd lost his mind.

"But, Bill, there's no way. . ."

"Don't argue with me. We have to hurry. Go pack a bag."

I packed a bag. The first thing he did was buy me an airline ticket. Then, we began the cumbersome task of getting together all the necessary documents for my leaving the country. We were United States citizens living in Brazil on permanent resident visas. In order to leave, I had to be finger-printed, photographed, and cleared of any criminal activity. Bill had always been good at visas and passports and getting us through customs. He knew which documents I would need, which fees needed to be paid, which lines to stand in, which officials to bribe. The telegram came. It was dated November 4, 1977, addressed *"Damon Bapmis Curitiba, Parana."* It read, "MOTHER TERMINALLY ILL DOCTOR GIVES NO HOPE EMERGENCY COME." Bill was all business. I had always dreamed of the romantic. He had always given me the practical. I had chafed at the gifts he chose–steam irons and crock pots. That day, I was grateful for his no-nonsense approach to getting things done. By that time, Bill and I had been married twenty years. He was frantically filling out forms while I cried. Suddenly, he looked up at me and said, "Are your eyes blue or brown?"

I replied, "Blue, and that's just proof you haven't looked into my eyes for twenty years." We stepped up to the last window as the clerk on duty was closing. He shook his head. *"Volte amanha."* Come back tomorrow.

"E uma emergencia. A mae dela esta morrendo." My husband's Portuguese was flawless. "It's an emergency. Her mother is dying." The man gave us a cynical glance and continued

closing down for the day. Bill demanded to see his supervisor. We were astounded to discover that the supervisor was a deacon in our church. We had no idea he worked in this office. Bill explained our situation.

"*Ela tem passagaem?*" "Does she have a ticket?"

"Yes."

"Go."

Bill, giving me instruction all the way, drove the forty-five minutes to the airport just in time for me to grab my bag and get on the plane. He stood watching until my plane was out of sight. I saw him wave. My heart lifted. I was on my way to Knoxville. I flew Varig from Curitiba to Rio, Pan Am from Rio to Miami, and then stand-by on American from Miami to Knoxville. My brother met me at the Knoxville airport and drove me to West Hills. Within twenty-four hours from the time I left Curitiba, I was walking into my mother's bedroom.

"Well, hi, honey. What are you doing here?" My mother was dying. She knew it. She had expressed a desire to die in her own bed at home.

"Oh, I just thought I'd come see you." I sat beside her bed and held her hand.

"Mom, has anyone read the Bible to you?"

"No."

"What would you like to hear?"

"John fourteen."

I quoted from memory. "Let not your heart be troubled. You believe in God. Believe also in me. In my Father's house are many mansions. If it were not so, I would have told you. I go to prepare a place for you. And if I go, I will come again and receive you unto myself that where I am, there you may be also. My peace I give to you, not as the world gives, give I unto you. Let not your heart be troubled, neither let it be afraid."

She slipped into sleep or unconsciousness.

We were changing the sheets when Carolyn suddenly said, "Well, I'll be leaving tomorrow. Now that you're here, she won't want me anymore. I'm the one who has been here for a week cleaning up her crap." The resentment in her voice was unmistakable.

"Don't go, Carolyn. I know she wants you here. And it would kill daddy if you left. Please. We all need you."

There was no more talk of her departure.

Mark, our first-born, came over from Wake Forest with his guitar. He sat by her bed and played and sang the old hymns mom loved. She loved him. When he was fifteen, he had come back to the States alone to go to school. Mother had wanted him to live with her and daddy and go to school for the year until we got home on furlough. My father would not hear of it. She was already ill, and daddy felt it would be too much for her. None of our other relatives were able or willing to take Mark in, but my mother wanted him. I will always love her for that, if for no other reason. Just how it began, I'm not sure, but my father became jealous of mother's affection for Mark and the attention she gave him. We sent Mark to school at Harrison-Chilhowee Academy in Seymour, Tennessee, just outside Knoxville. He lived in a dorm.

My mother wanted Mark for the weekends. The doctor had forbidden her to drive. She asked daddy to drive out and get Mark on Friday evenings and take him back on Sunday afternoons. Daddy let it be known that it was a great inconvenience, continually grousing and complaining. There was no grandfatherly affection toward Mark. Because there was such love between my eldest and my mother, daddy made clear his dislike. How absurd is it for a seventy-four-year-old man to be jealous of a fifteen-year-old boy? Maybe my father saw his own star falling as Mark's was rising. Maybe my father envied Mark his life. Maybe, as my mother lay dying, my father faced his own mortality. In her later years, my mother had learned to stand up to my father. I'm sure she was not above taking some pleasure in the fact that he could no longer control her. She also took pleasure in doing what she could for Mark. She poured out her affection on him. She loved him, because he was my child. They had long talks together on the couch in the den, much as she and I had experienced on our last furlough. It was a sweet time for them both, the power of love at work. Now, as she was dying, he sat by her bed and sang to her, "Amazing Grace," "The Old Rugged Cross," "No, Never Alone." And his love kept her alive and listening for his song.

Sarah Ann came. She was Paul's child, my dear cousin. Mother loved her like her own. Ever since daddy and mother had moved to Knoxville in 1965, Sarah Ann had been a constant presence in their home. She and her Aunt Mary Lou would sit for hours on the couch in the den talking and laughing together. They were good for each other, and there was a deep love between them.

Uncle Paul, Sarah Ann's, dad came. He was my mother's sweet boy. When their mother died in childbirth, Paul was five and mama was eighteen. She became a mother to him. The love that bonded them was strong and deep. He sat beside her bed, solid, silent, and tender. He had lost Grace, his birth mother, at five. He was a grown man who had lost his father to a heart attack and his only son to leukemia. Now, he was losing his mother all over again. Paul sighed and thought, "Heaven gets sweeter every year." He thought of the old Stamps-Baxter hymn:

Precious mem'ries, unseen angels,
Sent from somewhere to my soul.
How they linger, ever near me,
And the sacred past unfold.
Precious father, loving mother,
Fly across the lonely years,
  And old home scenes of my childhood,
In fond memory appears.
Precious mem'ries, how they linger,
How they ever flood my soul,
In the stillness of the midnight,
Precious, sacred scenes unfold.

Donald came into the room. He had been in the house for a week and no one knew how long this dying would take.

"Mother, I have to go back to work. I must go. I love you, Mother."

"I love you, Donald." It was said with a look made of all sweet accord.

Paul looked at Donald and said, "That's really good-bye." And it was.

Mark went back to Wake Forest. I told him I would call him when it was all over. Don went back to Maryland, and we promised to call him as soon as she was gone. Daddy, Carolyn, and I remained to wait. Paul and Sarah Ann were there much of the time. Mother's Sunday School girls came. Daddy said there would be no visitors, but I managed to slip a couple of them back to her bedroom so they could say their good-byes. Ann came in from Oklahoma. People from the church were in and out with food and promises of prayer. The night before she died, she saw the tunnel and the light and her father, my Granddaddy Patterson, waiting at the end of it on the other side.

We gathered around her bed. She smiled.

I asked, "Mama, what do you see?"

She said, "I see heaven."

"Is it beautiful?"

"Beauty beyond beauty."

"And can you see Jesus?"

"Yes, and he's smiling at me." And then she began a litany of praise: "Blessed be the name of Jesus. Blessed be the name of Jesus. Blessed be the name of Jesus." I looked at my father.

"She is on her knees before the Lord."

The next day she left us to go to that beautiful land.

KNOXVILLE–NOVEMBER 1977

Daddy's brothers, Shep, Buns, and Milford, and his sister, Alda, came to Knoxville from Nebraska for the funeral. At daddy's house, before the memorial service, Carolyn kept them in stitches telling jokes. She could be wickedly funny. Paul and Willa Mae, my Aunt Bill, and Sarah Ann and her husband, Larry, were there, of course, listening to the guffaws with ill-concealed disapproval. Don and Mary drove in from Maryland. Don's son, Don Jr., came from Virginia, as did Ann from Oklahoma, sitting on the couch in the den, silent, dressed in black. Mark had arrived the night before. We conversed quietly in the back bedroom.

"Mom, when I drove into Knoxville last night, I went directly to the funeral home. When I went in, I walked by two rooms. They were dark and dim, and there were only a few people, crying, in each one. And then I looked down the hallway, and there was a spill of light and laughter coming from the room where grandmom was. All the church people were there. It sounded like a celebration and I thought, 'People are going to think someone mean and rich died.'"

It was the first time I had smiled that day.

The doorbell rang. When I opened it, I couldn't believe my eyes. Joe and Peggy Rapert and Barbara Moore were standing on my daddy's front porch. They had traveled all the way down to Knoxville from Northern Virginia. Peggy and Barbara were my friends from high school. We had all been in the Del Ray Baptist Church youth group together as kids. Barbara married the great love of my sister's life. Carolyn had never forgiven her for it.

Carolyn's son, Brad, drove to Knoxville from Fort Wayne. I remembered him and his younger brother, Brett, as beautiful blonde, blue-eyed boys of four and five. Brad was grown and married and the father of a baby girl. Where had the years gone?

The service was sweet and simple. Frances Prince played the organ. I listened to the hymns and the words would come to my mind as she played. I looked at her and nodded. She winked at me and modulated into "God Will Take Care of You."

Be not dismayed whate'er betide,

God will take care of you.

Beneath his wings of love abide,

God will take care of you.

I believed it, but there was going to be a huge hole in my life without my mother. She was stubborn. She was partial. She could give the cold shoulder like no one I had ever known. But she was loyal. And when she loved you, she would defend you to the death. To the death.

Someone sang "Amazing Grace." Jack Prince, pastor of West Hills Baptist Church, did his standard funeral sermon appropriate for anybody and everybody, which said nothing about who or what Mary Lou Patterson McBride had been. I could have hit him for that. We went out into the dull, grey, November day to the cemetery on Kingston Pike. Rain began to fall. The heavens were weeping for my mother.

Brad started for Fort Wayne that afternoon. At ten o'clock that night, he called. I answered the phone.

"Aunt Roberta, I'm on the road. The weather is really bad, but I want to come back to Knoxville. I have to talk to you and Granddaddy. I want what my grandmother had."

"Honey, you get off the road and get to a motel and drive in tomorrow. It's too dangerous out there for you to be driving back tonight. Promise?"

"I promise."

The next morning, daddy went out to get the paper and found Brad asleep in his car in the driveway. He had driven in at four in the morning and didn't want to bother anyone. He came into the house and asked his grandfather what it was about his grandmom. Daddy took his Bible and showed Brad the scriptures that tell of God's love. Brad stayed for a week, even after his mother had gone back home. He would get up in the middle of the night and want to talk. He would wake me up, and we would go into the kitchen. I made hot chocolate, and we would sit at mother's kitchen table. Brad was emotionally fragile and insecure, like his mother.

Funerals give closure. Friends gather. They bring their love and support and pies and casseroles. And then, it's over. Except for the cleaning out of personal things. Daddy asked us to clean out mother's belongings. He wanted them out the day after the memorial service.

Carolyn made the rules. "No one is going to come into this house except the three of us. Not Ann, not Paul, not Sarah Ann, not any of mother's friends. No one is going to get anything. Whatever mother had belongs to us and no one else."

Carolyn and I sat on the floor in our parents' bedroom dividing up the costume jewelry from mother's jewelry box. It reminded me of when we were children playing a card game. Carolyn made up the rules as we went along to favor her hand. If she had deuces, suddenly, deuces were wild. As we sat dividing up the jewelry, she managed to take whatever was of any value. Several of the pieces were those I had given to mother as gifts. She took mother's large diamond "because Donna was the only granddaughter, and she would eventually have it." I got mother's original wedding band with its minuscule stones, only because Carolyn didn't want it. I did walk away with something I valued deeply–the small gold oval with HHH on the front for Howard Henderson Hospital. On the back was engraved in script: Mary Lou Patterson 1932. It was the gold pin she wore on her nurse's cap.

While we were sorting out mother's things, the phone rang. It was Mark calling from Wake Forest. "Mom, I got back safely."

"Okay, honey. I'm glad you called."

"Mom, I have to tell you what I did before I left Knoxville."

"What, honey?"

"Well, I went by McDonald's, bought a Big Mac and a milk shake, and I went to the cemetery and sat at Grand-mom's grave. I ate my lunch, and I said my own special good-bye to her. Do you think she would have minded that I had a picnic?"

"Oh, honey, she would have just loved it." I didn't think I could cry anymore, but I laughed and cried at the thought of Mark sitting among the flowers eating a Big Mac. He did love his grandmom. And she loved him.

Ann came to me privately and asked if she could have mother's black wool coat. "I was with her when she bought it. I'd like something to remember her by."

I mentioned to Carolyn that Ann wanted the black coat. "It won't fit me, and you live in Florida, so I doubt you want it."

"I don't care. What we don't want goes to Goodwill. I am not giving Mother's things to anyone."

Carolyn was leaving to go back to Fort Wayne in two days. I would stay with daddy for a month and write thank you notes and fill his freezer with individual dinners he could heat up. Ruby Ryan, dear old friend, volunteered to take the clothes someone could use to her little church and the rest on to Good Will.

I called Ruby. "I have a small problem. You have all of mother's clothes. My Aunt Ann wanted the black wool coat. She and mother were together when mom bought it. I hate to ask you to dig through all that stuff, but would you? And, a huge favor: would you please mail it to my Aunt Ann in Edmond, Oklahoma." Ruby said she would be glad to do it. She was a trooper. Carolyn never knew that Ann got mother's black wool coat.

I had written the two hundred or so thank you notes. I had filled the freezer. The time was drawing near for me to go back to Brazil. Mark was at Wake Forest and Christmas was coming up. Mark had spent the last several Christmases with my parents. One day, my father looked at me and said, "I don't want Mark here for Christmas."

I was startled. "Well, that presents a problem. I have to make plans for him to go somewhere."

"Why do you have to make plans ? He could just stay right there on the college campus. What would be wrong with that?" My father's voice was getting belligerent.

"What's wrong with that, Daddy, is that no child should have to spend Christmas alone on a deserted campus. The whole place closes down. I think even the dorms are closed."

"Well, you'll just have to make other arrangements, because I don't want him here."

"Yes, I heard you say that."

This was Mark's payoff for having been so loved by his grandmother. I was dying inside, but didn't have the energy to get into it with my father. My mind raced.

I called Bill's parents in Amarillo. "I have a little problem. Mark needs a place to go for the Christmas holidays. I wonder if he can come out to see you all?"

There was a long pause. I heard hesitation on the other end of the line. The wind up and then the pitch: "Well, I don't think that would be a good idea. You know, you never know about the weather. Mark could get stuck out here and then he couldn't get back to school."

"Okay. Well, never mind. I'll make other arrangements."

I called my cousin, Sarah Ann. "Houston, we have a problem."

"What's wrong, Bertie?"

"Well, I've got to go back to Brazil and Daddy doesn't want Mark here for Christmas and his Texas grandparents tell me it's not a good idea for him to be out there. Could you put my kid up for the Christmas holidays?"

"Why sure, Bertie. You know we'd be glad to have Mark."

"I'll love you forever for this." Who was it that had mentioned to me the phrase "the myth of the loving grandparent?" I felt like Mark had just lost all four of his. I was in such pain that I didn't even have the energy to be furious.

FORT WAYNE, INDIANA/
BONITA BAY, FLORIDA

My sister was given to repetition. In the McBride clan, stories tended to be told and retold with evolving embellishments. Carolyn, however, did not embroider her stories. In fact, her retelling was, invariably, a word for word rendering, so that by the fiftieth time it sounded so rehearsed it was as if someone had pushed the 'play' button on a tape recorder. She was like an Amway salesman, or a candidate for political office who goes from city to city giving the same speech day after day. Carolyn told her stories indiscriminately, to anyone who would listen–her siblings, her children, various therapists, her hair stylist, her friends, the young man who cleaned her house. The details she shared were so personal and so shocking it gave the listener a sense of exclusivity. It was a way she had of being intimate. When Carolyn told and retold her stories, I always had the feeling that she thought if she told the story often enough, maybe, just maybe, this time, it would have a happy ending. It never did.

The theme of Carolyn's stories was her victimization–by her husband, by our parents, by life. Her monologues were punctuated by dramatic pauses, emphasized words, expansive gestures and uncanny mimicry.

(Raised eyebrows, lowered voice) "When Bob fights, he fights dirty. He will always end up by saying to me, (disdainful look, sarcastic tone of voice) '*Look* at you. *Nobody* loves you. I don't love you. Your *kids* don't love you. Your *own* (rising inflection, heavy emphasis) *parents* don't love you.' (Pause, hushed tone) I have heard him say it over and over again and I *always* end up having the same reaction. I just (sorrowful expression) *die* inside and I (dramatic hand gesture) *throw* myself across the bed and *juuust* (pause, emphasize) *sob* (head bowed). And I know it's true. Bob told me one time to pack my bags and go home and spend as much time as I needed to get it out of my system and just to *prove* to myself that he was right about my parents not loving me. So, I went home to visit. (Conspiratorial tone) Daddy would go off to work. Mother would be silent all day. We just didn't have anything to say to each other, but (staccato, rising and falling inflections, shoulders rising and falling alternately) *just* as *soon* as *daddy* walked *in* the door, it would be, '*Aren't we having a gooood time?*' So daddy never knew. While I was there, she was so mean to me that I *threw* myself across the bed and *juuust* (pause, dramatic emphasis) *sobbed*, and she stood in the doorway and said, (sarcastic tone) 'You always *could* cry at the drop of a hat.' I packed my suitcase and caught the next plane home. I just had to get *out* of there. And when I saw Bob waiting for me at the airport, I ran into his arms and I *juuust* (pause, heavy emphasis) *sobbed*."

She lived in chaos. The man she married was the adult child of an alcoholic father. Bob had worked to earn his own support from the time he was a child of ten. He was smart. He was charming. He was a hustler. Everything he touched turned to money. When he walked into his favorite bar, people would gather around him from all corners of the room. He drew people to himself like a magnet. He fascinated, like a snake charmer. He was as erratic and volatile as the wife he married. And he was utterly controlling. He and Carolyn were a perfect couple. She was a bottomless pit of need for love and had substituted material objects for the affection she craved. He provided every material thing that anyone could dream up. All he asked in return was absolute obedience. Together, they produced four beautiful, intelligent, emotionally starved children.

CARNEGIE–1935

The battle between Mary Lou and the two children was epic. Not only had they lost their mother, but also, suddenly, there appeared in her place, a head nurse. Whereas Keith had been indulgent and tender, Mary Lou was not inclined to tolerate any foolishness. When she moved in, Donald asked, "What shall we call her?"

Don looked at his new wife. His answer was immediate. "You'll call her 'Mother.'"

Mary Lou said, "If they want to call me 'Mary Lou,' I don't mind."

"Nonsense," said Don. "They'll call you 'Mother.'"

Bed time was established, and there were no exceptions. Meals were nourishing, plentiful, and served on time. If the children didn't eat what was put before them, their plates were taken away, and they had nothing to eat until the next meal was on the table. Whereas their first mother would get them a drink of water when they wanted one, this mother pushed a step stool up to the kitchen sink and taught them to get their own drink. They were required to wash their hands before meals without being reminded. Mary Lou was a disciplinarian. She did not believe in sparing the rod. If Carolyn pitched a hissy and fell on the floor and held her breath until she turned blue, Mary Lou picked her up and spanked her bottom. Once, Donald and his little friend, Billy, were sitting on the back porch. Billy said, "I liked your other mother better than this one." Mary Lou overheard it and, thinking Donald had made the remark, she walked out onto the porch, picked

Donald up, and spanked him. Mary Lou was taking no guff.

Mary Lou was tired. She was tired of the McGregors undermining everything she tried to do to impose some order on the chaos in her new family. She was tired of their constantly reminding the children that they were poor little motherless tykes. She was tired of the children's disobedience. She was already beginning to get tired of Don's never being around and leaving her with all the heavy lifting. Ever since her own mother's death, she had done nothing but take care of kids. The only escape from it was nurse's training and her work at Howard Henderson. Some days she couldn't believe she had given up being a surgical nurse to take on Don's kids. What had she been thinking? She was tired, and she had no sympathy, and she had no patience.

Donald was a little lost soul. He was old enough to remember life before Keith's death. Big as he was, his mama would take him up on her lap and rock him. Her hands were gentle. Her voice was like honey. She didn't care if the house was clean or dinner was on the table. The children came first, always. Donald felt utterly safe and protected when his mama was there. With Mary Lou in his life, he dreamed that Keith was an angel. In his dream, she told him that she loved him. He would reach out to her, but she was far away. Sometimes, in the moment after waking, he thought he heard her footsteps outside his bedroom door. And then, he knew all over again that she was gone. He longed for her to come back to him and rock him again in the old rocking chair. Sometimes, he would stand and look at the chair and feel like crying. But if the tears came, he would quickly wipe them away. He would square his thin little shoulders and raise his chin. He knew big boys weren't supposed to cry, and the adults around him often reminded him that he was a big boy. "A big boy like you should know how to tie his shoes." "You're a big boy. Sit up at the table and cut your own meat." "Big boys don't act like babies." At six, he became a realist. He understood that his mother was never coming back, and life would never be the same. He wished he could make life right again. He knew that it would never be right again.

Donald felt a responsibility to help his little sister. He didn't like it when she had tantrums, but with primal knowledge and a child's wisdom, he knew she did those things because she was afraid. He knew it, because he knew his own fear. Sometimes, they held each other for comfort.

When their mother died, they lost their father, as well. Or, maybe they had never had him in the first place. When Keith died, they knew, on some elemental level, that it was not by her choice. They knew she would come back if she could. But it was different with their father. He betrayed them. How could he stand by and not only let this interloper do these terrible things, but applaud her while she did them? The children needed discipline, it's true, but they needed love more. Mary Lou became the ogre. The children became the victims. Don reestablished his custom of having a drink every evening with Harry Jolly.

$\mathscr{C}$ARNEGIE–1936

$\mathcal{M}$ary Lou wanted a baby. She had been taking care of other people's children long enough–first her own siblings, and then Don's children. She longed for a child of her own. The months passed. In spite of frequent and ardent efforts, she did not conceive. She made an appointment with the doctor. When he spoke with her in his office after examining her, he did not offer her much hope.

"The uterus is tipped–turned in the wrong direction. You have a naturally built in system of birth control. You are perfectly normal in every respect. It is just highly unlikely that you will ever be able to conceive."

She went home to tell Don the news. He tried to be sympathetic, but found it difficult. "We already have two children. I know you want a baby of your own, but I'm not sure we could even afford another child. Can't you be happy with what we have?"

Mary Lou looked at him in astonishment. "We may have two children here under this roof, but you have three children–or have you forgotten that baby girl over at the Anderson's? Angry, fretful tears pooled in her eyes. "You have no idea what it means for a woman to give birth to a child of the man she loves. I want to give you a child. I want you to give me one, and if I can't have my own, I would be glad to settle for the one you gave away." She turned from him. Taking a deep breath, she spoke more calmly. "I've been thinking about it for some time now, and after what the doctor told me today, I have decided. I want to go get her."

"Now, wait just a minute. We've got to give this some thought. First of all, she has never known any other parents but May and Melford Anderson, so it might be hard on her. She has been with them for over a year and a half–since she was six weeks old. And besides, I have practically promised them they can adopt her. We have to think what effect it would have on Donald and Carolyn. And besides that, we can't afford another child. I just don't know. Let me think about it."

Mary Lou nodded. "Think about it all you want, but she's your child. I can't understand how you could just give her away."

Mary Lou thought of me as the underdog. She said over and over again, "I'm for the underdog." I was the child daddy had discarded. The McGregors favored the older two children and either ignored me or blamed me. Ironically, the result was that Mary Lou created new underdogs in Donald and Carolyn. In her effort to rescue me, she denigrated them. She seemed to look upon the older two children as the burdens, a part of the package deal, that came with her marriage to daddy. She used sarcasm, the silent treatment, and threats. She was the informer. "Just wait until your daddy gets home" was her oft repeated refrain. When daddy arrived home from work, she met him at the door with a list of the crimes the children had committed that day. Daddy would whip off his belt, herd the kids into the bathroom, require them to hold onto the edge of the bathtub, and whale away. He often drew blood. Sometimes, as I got older, I was included, but I did not get the kind of abuse that my siblings suffered. That kind of beating always sent Carolyn first, into hysterical crying, and then into hateful resentment. Donald got to the place where he refused to cry. He would grit his teeth and glare at daddy. That fueled daddy's rage. When our father had a belt in his hand, he never knew when to stop. I am convinced that the reason I was such a good little girl is that I was terrified into compliance. I admired my brother, who could take it and not cry. I knew that after Carolyn got a beating, she would dump her hate on me. I lived much of my life afraid of daddy's temper, and then afraid of Carolyn's.

Oklahoma City–1941

In 1941 daddy had paid off his debts, and he bought a house

on Twenty-fourth Street. Other than paying a mortgage instead of renting, our lives did not change much. Daddy had abdicated any responsibility for child rearing, except for meting out punishment. Child rearing was left to Mary Lou. She was not a playmate—not ever. She was the authority figure in our home. Motive did not matter. Accidents were punished right along with sins. Even if we didn't mean to do something, we were punished. Carolyn was the scapegoat of our family. If anything went wrong, she was the first to be blamed. And whatever went wrong had to be someone's fault. Once Carolyn carried a freshly frosted chocolate cake from kitchen counter to the table. Mother yelled, "Don't drop it." And of course, she did. Carolyn was a nervous child, given to hysterics. No wonder.

Mother was sick and tired much of the time. She was the picture of a martyr. When we would ask permission to go to someone's house to play, she would sigh deeply and say reluctantly, "I guess so." We knew that she was displeased again. My sister reacted to her with resentment. My brother reacted by acting out. I reacted by tap dancing. I learned early that if I could keep my parents entertained, I would be safe. I became "the cute one, the good one, the smart one." I brought credit to my parents. I was afraid not to. Carolyn and Donald were "the bad ones, the difficult ones, the dumb ones." Sarcasm was standard fare. "Pretty is as pretty does." "Who asked you?" "If I want your opinion, I'll ask you for it." "As long as you put your feet under my table, you will do as I say." "Your name is IKE—it stands for 'I know everything.'" "Maybe we should call her IT-IKE—'I think I know everything.'" If someone wet the bed (and we all did), we were called "pee-cats." If the two older children brought home a report card with average or below average grades, there was never a word of encouragement, nor was there promise of help. I remember once when Carolyn was in junior high, she got an A in gym and Cs in her other courses. Daddy said, "Well, I see you are A-one hotsy-totsy in gym class. And in everything else you aren't so great. You never apply yourself. What have I done to have a kid like you?" What both my brother and sister heard was how stupid and lazy they were. If a child gets enough of that, over the years, he will begin to believe it.

ALEXANDRIA, VIRGINIA–1948

I do remember one time I talked back to my father. I must have been thirteen. I skipped a piano lesson and went bike riding with my friend, Nancy Nevin—an uncharacteristically irresponsible thing for me to do. When daddy yelled that he had to pay for those lessons whether or not I showed up, he ended his speech with, "You just let Nancy lead you around by the nose. How did you get so stupid?" I said, "Maybe I took after my father." The wrath of God descended. Mother looked on approvingly. "I wondered if you were going to let her get by with that." He didn't. And mostly, I was too scared to fight back.

OKLAHOMA CITY–1944

Donald got into real trouble. He was out before daylight with his paper route. He had moved out of our house into the room attached to the garage. We grandly called it the "servant's quarters." Living there gave him too much freedom and opportunity to slip out at all hours. He and his friends began to steal cars and take them on joy rides. They were caught on more than one occasion. On the same day daddy was honored with an appointment as the new chairman of the Oklahoma Water Resources Board, Donald was arrested for stealing cars. Both items appeared in *The Daily Oklahoman*. The judge commented to daddy when Donald was sentenced, "If you are a failure as a father, no matter what honors you receive, you are a failure." That didn't set too well with daddy.

When Donald was twelve, our Graddaddy McGregor died. That left my brother without an emotional anchor. As far as I can remember, daddy never took Donald fishing. He never played ball with him. If it were not for our uncles, Donald would not have had any of those father-son activities. Uncle Sam, Ann's husband, took him hunting and fishing. Uncle Ray let him ride horses. Uncle Shep treated him like one of his own. All daddy knew to do with him was to send him away–to Uncle Ray's farm near Carnegie for the summer, to Uncle Shep's in Nebraska for a school year.

The summer Donald was fifteen, daddy got him a job with the State Highway Department on a survey crew in Tulsa. Donald stayed by himself in a boardinghouse. He was on his own, paying his rent and buying his meals. At the end of that summer, he went back to Oklahoma City and enrolled in Central High School. He worked part time in a grocery store across the street from the school. He did not do well academically, because he cut class and didn't study. When he went back to school after a long absence, he was asked to read aloud in English class. He pronounced 'Penelope' as 'pena-lope.' When the students laughed, he dropped out of school, lied about his age, and joined the United States Army. Daddy, relieved, said that it would "make a man of him." Before Donald's seventeenth birthday, with a Thompson sub-machine gun in hand, he was guarding Hermann Goering, Rudolph Hess, and Franz Von Papen at the Palace of Justice during the trials of the German war criminals at Nurenberg. He was barely more than a child. For all practical purposes, when he left home at sixteen, he never returned.

$\mathcal{C}$ARNEGIE–1936

Charles adored his baby sister. He proudly displayed her to his friends. He would put her in the basket of his bicycle and delight in her shrieks of joy as, together, they bounced over the ruts in the dirt road. When she was just over a year old, Charles decided he would teach her to talk. He would say a word over and over. She would look at him with big eyes, as silent as a sphinx. She found him interesting and entertaining.

Wherever May went, the baby went. She took her to the worship services at church, Sunday morning and Sunday night. Other mothers might have to take their children out for disrupting the service. May was proud that she never had to take her child out. They were a perfect pair—mother and child, utterly content in each other's presence. When May taught the older children in Vacation Bible School, she pulled the crib up by the doorway and allowed the boys and girls to entertain the toddler. When May was in the kitchen at home, the crib was pulled into the doorway where the baby could be safe and still feel connected to her. It was a tender symbiosis.

Melford idolized the child. She crowed happily whenever he came into the room. He would carry her out to the back of their lot where he kept his tools in the shed. When he set up his sawhorses and got out his saw, she sat on the cement sidewalk and watched. She played in the sawdust like other children play in sand. And when he created curly shavings of pine that fell from under the plane, she lifted her chubby hands to catch them, and laughing, put them in her hair.

CARNEGIE–1993

May looked at me with love as she recalled that early time. "Oh, honey, we did love you so much. Charles would ride you all over on his bicycle, and you would laugh. Charles wanted you to learn to talk. He took you outside at night and pointed up at the moon. 'Moon, moon,' he would say. He was trying to teach you to say 'moon.'"

Suddenly, breathlessly, I said, "Your husband was a carpenter."

"Yes."

"I played in the sawdust."

"Yes."

"I put the wood curls in my hair."

"Yes."

"We lived in this house."

"Yes. We built this house, Melford and I. Yes, you lived here with us. And you called me 'Mama' and you called him 'Papa.' Yes, it was here. And then, they came to get you."

"It must have been hard for you."

"Oh, honey, I thought I would die. After you were gone, for months, I would be working in my garden, and I would hear a baby cry. I would be halfway to the house before I realized there was no baby. Oh, yes. I thought I would die."

Carnegie—1936

Mary Lou put the roast in the oven. It would be done by the time church was over. Today was an important day. She had visited May Anderson in her home and held the baby. They had a nice talk and then, Mary Lou had invited them all over for Sunday dinner. Yesterday, she had scrubbed the house and the children clean, and warned everyone to be on their best behavior. Company was coming for dinner.

Charles and Melford were dressed in their Sunday best. They were about as uncomfortable as they could be. Their shoes were shined and their ties were neatly tied. Melford carried the baby's walker. May carried the baby up the short walkway to the door. Don greeted them, invited them all in, and encouraged Charles and Melford to take off their coats and ties. May put the baby in her walker. Mary Lou hurried in from the kitchen to greet her guests. She had put yellow roses in a bowl on the coffee table. Seeing the baby, she immediately began to remove the vase.

"Don't worry about the flowers. She won't bother them." May let the little one smell the bouquet. "Flower. Pretty flower," May crooned. The child stopped, stuck her nose into a rose, lost interest, and went to Melford.

Dinner went well. The food was delicious. The children were well behaved. The conversation was lively. Just as it was time for the Andersons to leave, Don spoke to May and Melford.

"I want you to know how grateful I am that you have taken such good care of Roberta." May's heart stopped. "Harry Jolly has put me in touch with the governor's office in Oklahoma City, and I may be looking at a new job there.

I don't know yet, for sure, that it will even happen, but we have to think about what we are going to do about this baby. We won't make any sudden moves, so it's not going to happen right away, but you need to be thinking about it now."

Melford and May nodded mutely. Charles didn't understand. "You mean you are going to take her away from us?"

"Oh, you can visit her any time you want. You are always welcome here, Charles, you know that. And, of course, your mother and daddy, too."

How they got from Don's house to their own, none of them knew. The only happy one in the house that day was the baby, and her happiness was born of blissful ignorance.

Within weeks, they set a day to come to get her. May lived with dread. Her eyes followed the toddler's every move as if to memorize each moment. May wanted to hold up her hands and stop time, but time seeped, and then rushed, through her fingers. On the inevitable day, May packed the baby's clothes and bathed and dressed her for the short journey across town and out of their lives forever. Don drove up in his car. May could see that he was alone. He came into the house through the kitchen door.

"I guess this is not the time for small talk. I've come for the baby."

"I know. She's all ready."

May handed him the little suitcase full of baby clothes. He reached for the child. When Don took the baby from May's arms, her cry of terror matched the anguish in May's heart. Don moved quickly. He turned to May.

"Thanks for everything. She'll be okay. The quicker I do this, the better for everyone." He carried the screaming child to his car, and they were gone.

May sat at her kitchen table, her head in her hands,

praying for strength to take the next breath. She neither ate nor slept for three days. "Oh, God, help me. Help my baby. Oh, God, be Thou my strength in this time of trouble. Oh God, help me bear this." Neither Melford nor Charles could assuage her grief. She was every mother. She was Rachel weeping for her children.

To father a child means to beget. To mother a child means to nurture, love, protect, teach, guide, feed, clothe, bathe, soothe, comfort, tend, and nourish. To father a child is to contribute a sperm. To mother a child has nothing to do with contributing an egg. To mother a child is to see to the child's emotional, physical, psychological, social, and spiritual well-being. Some fathers mother children. Some mothers do not. Mothering at its best involves nourishment of the spirit as well as the body. The umbilical cord that reaches from mother to child carries physical nourishment. But other unbreakable cords bind us: cords of love and commitment that are life giving and life enhancing.

Charles rode his bicycle to see his baby sister after school. Mary Lou greeted him cordially and assured him that he could come visit any time. He came every day. It was not the same. It was never the same. After three weeks, May went to visit. The baby had a fever. In all the time she had been with May, the child had not been sick. Not one day. Not once. May tried to talk to her, but she turned her wan little face to the wall. Then, Don took the job in Oklahoma City, and they were gone.

CARNEGIE–1993

May went into her bedroom and brought out a small photograph in an old fashioned glass frame. It was a studio sepia of a small girl.

"That's a picture of me. I've never seen it before, but I recognize it as a picture of me."

"This is how you looked when they took you away from me."

I looked long at the child me. I was a dead ringer for Shirley Temple. I had a mass of curly hair parted on the right, a huge bow perched on top of the hair on the left. I had a button nose, and dimpled baby hands. I was seated on a brocade covered bench in the obligatory pose: right leg bent so that the right ankle was under the left knee. I was wearing a freshly ironed print cotton dress with piping around the collar and the short sleeves. I had on white sandals with three straps across the instep and what looks to be colored socks. Somehow, I do not look like I am about to burst into a rendition of "On the Good Ship Lollipop." I look anxious and depressed and sober as a judge.

"They came to take you away." May's voice broke. "Your daddy was going to let us adopt you, but your stepmother couldn't have children, so they came and got you."

"That must have been hard for you."

"Oh, honey, I thought I would die. When I had you, wherever I went, you went. Then they came to get you. I visited you in your new home. You had a fever. You had never been sick when you were with me. When I came to see you, you wouldn't look at me. You were so sad. Yes, and so was I. For all that summer, I would be out weeding the garden, and I was sure I heard you cry. It was a hard time."

$\mathscr{C}$ARNEGIE–1994

$\mathscr{B}$ill and I were on our way to Amarillo. We had spent the night at Ann's in Edmond. She had packed crackers and grape juice for us. We were going to stop at Mrs. Anderson's house and celebrate communion. I had my Bible and had marked some passages for Bill to read. I would have conducted the ritual myself, but I knew that she would be scandalized by a woman's doing what God meant for men to do. At ninety-three, we are not into women's ordination. We have pictures of her that day. She was frail. It had been a long time since she had participated in communion. She called it "The Lord's Supper."

Bill read. At times his voice faltered. "And Jesus took the bread and broke it saying, 'This is my body broken for you. Take, eat.' The three of us ate a bit of cracker. "And taking the cup, he blessed it saying, 'This is my blood of the New Covenant, shed for many for the remission of sins. Drink ye all of it.'" We drank our juice from jelly glasses. "'As oft as ye eat this bread and drink this cup, ye do shew forth the Lord's death 'til he come. Do this in remembrance of me.'" We looked at each other and smiled. It was a sweet time of fellowship.

CARNEGIE—1936

At six, Donald accepted the baby as his new sister. He hadn't been too enthusiastic when they broke the news to him, but he thought about it and decided it was okay. Carolyn hated her before the day she was carried into the house. The baby was just one more thing that would steal the love that was rightfully hers. First a stepmother and now this.

Donald climbed the hog wire fence between the back yard and the alley. He and Billy Lee were going to the elementary school to slide down the big pipe fire escape. He looked over his shoulder. Carolyn was calling to him.

"I'm going with you, Donald. Wait for me."

"No, Carolyn. You're too little. You go back. Girls can't play with us." He couldn't be bothered with a four-year-old sister this day. Donald ran to the corner, met Billy, and the two boys were off toward the school building.

Carolyn was determined. She struggled to climb the fence. With great effort, she managed to reach the top. It was then that her foot caught in the topmost wire square. She flailed her arms, found nothing to hold onto and lost her balance. The child was catapulted into the alley. She fell with all her weight on her knee, and her knee struck the glass of a broken fruit jar. Her screams brought Mary Lou running. When Mary Lou saw the depth of the cut and the amount of blood, she raced back to the house, grabbed a pad from the doll bed, put Carolyn on it and carried her the three blocks to the hospital.

The wound was deep. It required twenty-six stitches and left a scar the size and shape of a Brock's orange slice. She carried it all her life. Curiously, Carolyn had a clear memory of the fall and of the cut, but all her life she believed it had been Keith who rescued her and carried her to the hospital. Years later, when Carolyn was an adult, as we were gathered at mother and daddy's house in Knoxville, someone mentioned the scar. Carolyn told the story of how Keith had rushed her to the emergency room.

Mary Lou listened. She said quietly, "No, Carolyn. You were four when that happened. I'm the one who carried you to the hospital."

"Are you sure?" Carolyn was shocked.

"Well, of course I'm sure."

Carolyn was shaken. It was Mary Lou and not Keith. How could she have been so mistaken? The scar had been visible proof of Keith's love for her. She had worn it like a talisman. She could touch it with her fingers and remember that it was her first mother who scooped her up and anxiously hovered over her. The scar on her knee was an outward sign of the inner scar she carried all of her life. She was so sure in her mind that it had been Keith, her beautiful lost mother, who had been present that day. She thought of her mother as a guardian angel whose wings whispered to her just before she slept. Carolyn was the child, frightened and running through the dark night, but Keith was the guiding force who would, in some fair land, provide all wisdom, all nurture, all love. It was Keith who had carried her in her womb and then, so briefly, in her arms. It was Mary Lou who carried her to the hospital that day so long ago, when Carolyn was hurt. The scar had always been to Carolyn, living proof that her mother had, indeed, held her close and loved her before conscious memory.

ALEXANDRIA, VIRGINIA–1947

In September of 1946, right after the war, we moved to Alexandria, Virginia when daddy took the job of Secretary Manager of the National Reclamation Association, awaiting Bob Kerr's anticipated run for the United States Senate in 1948. He worked in Washington, across the Potomac River. We lived on Hickory Street just off Mount Ida in a house my father described as a cracker box set on end, a testimony to the post war housing shortage. At the foot of the hill, a block down from our house, lay the playground of Mount Vernon Elementary School. I had finished sixth grade there in June. With the arrival of fall, I had just begun seventh grade at George Washington High School.

It was Indian summer. The trees were beginning to show

touches of yellow and red and brown, but the weather was still not cold enough for a jacket. In an effort to prolong summer, kids gathered in the pale late afternoon sunshine with skates and basketballs at Mount Vernon School. We played on the huge square surfaced in smooth cement, a perfect place to roller skate.

Carolyn had taken her shoe skates and gone on down the hill. I had to finish piano practice. After the last Hannon finger exercise, I put my music in the piano bench, closed the lid over the piano keys, and went upstairs to get my skates out of the closet I shared with my sister. The red felt bolero with the silver studs caught my eye. It belonged to Carolyn and I knew it was off limits to me, but I couldn't resist it. I put it on—a fatal mistake in judgment as it turned out. I looked good in my jeans, my white shirt, and Carolyn's red bolero. I fluffed my shoulder length hair and stopped to preen for a moment before the mirror. Picking up my skates, I walked down the hill.

I put my skates on and stood, just ready to push off. Suddenly, Carolyn skated into me with the force of a fullback tackling an opponent. I fell, sprawling. She screamed at me, "That's my bolero. You're a thief. Keep your hands off my things." She punched me over and over again, pulled my hair, scratched my face with her fingernails, and tore the bolero off my back. Kids gathered around in awe. She yanked the bolero off me and skated away with it.

My nose was bleeding. I tasted blood and tears. Weeping, I removed my skates and started toward home, humiliated, sickened, and shaken. I had seen raw hatred in my sister's face. I had seen it before, but this time, my friends saw it, too.

Mama dabbed at the scratches on my cheek with burning iodine.

"You know better than to take things without asking.

Don't ever do it again."

It was not likely.

Oklahoma City—1937

I don't have to mind you. You're not my mother. Nana said."
Carolyn stuck out her chin belligerently.

"You do have to mind me, missy. I may not be your mother,
but I'm all you have. And you will mind me, no matter what
your nana says."

"No, I won't." Mary Lou swatted her on the behind. "You
will not talk to me like that."

Carolyn cried. "I want my mama back. My mama was
nice. You're mean."

Mary Lou picked her up and put her in a chair. "Yes, I am
mean. You just sit here until you can be a good girl." At the
tender age of five, Carolyn began to think of herself as a bad
girl. She wondered if she would have to sit in that chair for the
rest of her life. In a way, she did.

Carolyn was a strong-willed child—and a fighter. If she was
crossed, she would kick and scream. She desperately wanted to
be loved. The more she wanted love, the more she demanded.
The more she demanded, the harder the discipline with
the result that she felt loved even less. She was labeled "the
problem child." Somewhere deep within her, she resolved very
early that she would get love. She was greedy for it. Material
objects began to represent love. When she was a child, she was
greedy for candy, or ice cream, or nickels and dimes. Gimme,
gimme, gimme.

Once, at children's church at Trinity, the boys and girls
competed for two chalk drawings. Carolyn won one of them,

but it was not the one she wanted. She was furious, stamped her feet, and threw such a fit, that the child who had won the prettier of the two drawings, gave up and gave hers to Carolyn. All of the kids saw her as a fierce competitor and gave her a wide berth. As she grew, the objects she coveted were more sophisticated, but the desire was the same–the desire for love. Her teachers at school invariably wrote: Carolyn does not work up to her potential. Carolyn is bright, but does not concentrate on her work. Carolyn needs to change her attitude.

Carnegie–1938

Effie and R.K. were on their way back home from having the children all summer. By this time, the McGregors lived in Temple, Texas, and Don and Mary Lou lived in Oklahoma City. Effie and R.K. stopped in Carnegie to go to the cemetery. They drove south out of town, turned east, and drove the mile-and-a-half until they found the cemetery and the second iron gate. R.K. parked just inside the entrance by the big cedar tree.

"We are going to take you to your mother's grave, children." Effie had already begun to cry. "Oh, I'll never get over losing your mother. She was so wonderful. She was so good. She was so beautiful. She loved you both so much."

R.K. stood with the children beside Keith's grave. The flat stone, flush with the grass, was inscribed simply, "Mrs. Don McBride 1906-1935." The grave lay beside other plots still empty and waiting. One would be R.K.'s final resting place. The other one was for Effie. R.K. bent down to brush dirt from the stone. "She was a good daughter to us and a good mother to you children." His eyes filled with tears. "I do miss her so much."

Donald began to cry. "I wish I had my mother back." Carolyn joined in.

"I want my mama. I loved my mama. Why did my mama have to go to heaven?"

Effie was weeping. Great sobs shook her frame. "She was such a precious mother. She was your real mother. The one at home is not your real mother, and you do not have to mind her. She can't tell you what to do. Keith was your real mother."

Donald said it again. "I wish we had her back with us."

R.K. put his arms around the little boy. "I do too, honey. We all do." The four of them stood around the grave, heartbroken and weeping together.

The children were on emotional overload.

Texas/Tennessee—1937-1941

Carolyn and Donald loved the summers. Summer meant being with Nana and Papa. Summers meant being petted and made over. Nana was in bed a lot. She was not well. The children tip-toed inside the house, because Nana had headaches. Papa was not sick. He was pastor of the church. Donald and Carolyn watched him write sermons on his Underwood typewriter. They went with him sometimes when he visited sick people. He took them to Vacation Bible School. Papa did all of the house cleaning and cooked dinner. One summer he built a barbecue grill in the back yard, and he let the children help. Donald could use Papa's tools any time he wanted. He nailed two sticks together in the form of an airplane and ran around the yard, holding it high, making airplane noises. Once, from scrap lumber Papa had given him, he built himself a pulpit like Papa's, and he stood behind it and preached. Papa carried a pocket knife with a yellow handle. Donald could say to Papa, "Let me borrow your pocket knife," and Papa would always let him use it with the warning, "Now, don't cut yourself." Papa had always loved Donald. When Donald was very young, he would have convulsions. Papa would put him in a bathtub of water, and he would say to himself as he drew the water, "Not too hot, Mac. Not too hot." Papa had always taken care of Donald.

One summer, when the children visited, Papa built a swing. One day, a little boy Carolyn was sweet on had come to visit. She wore a circle skirt Nana had made for her. When she stood up to pump on the swing, the snap popped open and her skirt dropped off. Oh, the humiliation of it all! They went to church on Sundays, and everyone there came by to say what sweet grandchildren Brother Mac had. Carolyn and Donald loved summers with their McGregor grandparents. They never wanted to go back to Oklahoma.

While the older children were with their McGregor grandparents in Texas, Mary Lou and Ann and I would go home to Tennessee for a month. Sometimes, daddy would drive from Oklahoma, drop us off, stay a few days and then go back to work. Sometimes, we would take the train and Uncle Paul would meet us at Sweetwater and drive us over to Tellico.

Granddaddy Patterson's house was an ideal place for a child. A little way down the road was a branch to wade in and to dam up with mud and rocks. A spring of sweet water ran through it. A dipper was hung on the rock, so that anyone who went by there could get a drink of water. Granddaddy had his men keep that spring cleaned out and free of overgrowth. The hayloft down at the barn was there for the sole purpose of delighting a child. Jumping from the rafters into a huge mound of hay over and over again could take an afternoon. The orchard was full of apples. Sliced tomatoes, bread, mayonnaise, and salt and pepper made a great afternoon snack. Just inside the kitchen door was a bucket and a dipper for drinking. At dinner time, my granddaddy would let me eat as many roasting ears of corn as I wanted. Corn on the cob was a special summer treat in those pre-freezer days. The house was huge with high ceilinged bedrooms and iron bedsteads covered with hand made quilts. There were cool places for reading or dreaming—on the porch swing or under a tree. The store on wheels would come by—a huge peddler's pack of a truck. The back doors would be thrown open and mama could buy all kinds of things—thread, coffee, sugar, shoes, fabric, ready-made dresses. The mail truck came by every other day. It was back in the time when people still wrote letters. If mama got a letter from daddy, she would announce, "Well, I got a hearing from my man today." She didn't talk like that at home, but in Tellico, she talked "Tennessee talk." My job for the summer was to run down the huge front lawn to the mailbox by the fence at the roadside for the mail. Hollyhocks, angel's trumpets, four o'clocks, and cannas grew all along the fence. Morning glories and honeysuckle and wild roses climbed everywhere and perfumed the hot summer air. On Sundays, Uncle Paul would come and take us swimming in the river, or we would stay home, cut a watermelon, and toss horseshoes. I loved summers at Granddaddy Patterson's. I hated to go back home.

One summer, we traveled to Tennessee by train. Daddy made reservations for Mary Lou, Ann, and me on the Rocket. Between Oklahoma City and Knoxville, it stopped only in Little Rock, Memphis, and Nashville. We would sleep in the Pullman car and eat in the dining car. My Uncle Paul would pick us up at the Knoxville depot. When we arrived in Little

Rock, we learned that the Rocket had become a troop train, and we were transferred to a milk train that stopped at every crossroad and pig trail. I remember the soldiers standing in the aisles. We insisted on standing while they got some rest. They were nice, like the boys we had known at Trinity. I sat on a suitcase in the aisle most of that trip. It was a great adventure.

Another summer, during the war years when everything was rationed, daddy had saved enough coupons for gasoline and tires so that we could drive to Tennessee. The first night on the road, we stopped at a tourist home. Before we went to bed, Ann washed out her rather large rayon step-ins in the bathroom sink. I stood and watched her swish the silky garment in the soap suds, rinse out the soap, wring out the excess water, and find a place on the shower rod that would serve as a clothes line for the night. My Aunt Ann had a tiny waist and broad hips. I remember the panties she washed were of a peachy, orange hue. They were snug around the waist, but the legs hung loosely, reaching almost to the knees. I was sure they were the kind worn by Mrs. Eleanor Roosevelt, the wife of our President. At any rate, Ann's underwear was not dry the next morning. All day long, until they were dry, she cheerfully waved them out of our car window at the caravans of army troop trucks we passed on the highway. It was her contribution to the war effort. She saw it as a way to bolster morale. Hundreds of soldiers cheered mightily at Ann and her fluttering standard. My father slumped lower and lower into the front seat behind the wheel. I giggled and giggled. My mother kept saying, "Ann, for goodness sake. Behave yourself." But my Aunt Ann never did.

I remember those summers as being free from family conflict. I remember it as a relief.

CARNEGIE–1993

After we discovered May Anderson in January, Carolyn called.

"We have to go back to Oklahoma. I want to order a large family marker for the McGregor plot. I was just appalled that the information on the stones was so sketchy and the stones were so small. Donald and I have just about found all the information we need on Effie and R.K. Don has Effie's death certificate, and I have found R.K.'s. When can you go?"

"Give me a chance to look at my calendar, and I'll call you back."

We decided on a trip in late May. Donald would not be able to go, but we wanted to get this done. Don assured us that he would trust our judgment. We would split the cost of the monument three ways.

Carolyn and I met in Oklahoma City and drove down to Carnegie. The trip was pleasant. When we got together in those days, we never ran out of things to say to each other. Carolyn told me the latest about her family—who was getting married, who was getting divorced, who was in her good graces, and who was not. Her energy was contagious. I always felt a surge of adrenalin in her presence. She was so much like our father—excited and exciting—and sometimes, dangerous.

"I want to go by *The Carnegie Herald* office and find out if they keep old copies of the paper from the twenties and thirties. And we need to go by the funeral home to see about ordering the stone. What's the name of it?"

"Pitcher-Hackney Funeral Home. It's down catty corner from the church."

"Yeah, I know where it is. I just couldn't remember the

name of it."

We drove into Carnegie. By now the town looked familiar.

"Funeral home first, okay?"

"That's okay with me."

Carolyn headed down Main, passing all the places we had seen in January. Winter brown had given way to spring green. The wind had changed from bone-chilling to pleasant. We parked in front of the Funeral Home, a house which had been enlarged and remodeled. We climbed the steep front steps and walked into the reception area. A sweet-faced young woman greeted us.

Carolyn explained our situation. "I really don't know how to go about this, but we're hoping you can help us."

"I'll certainly try. My name is Martha Hackney. And you are . . .?"

"Carolyn Brown. This is my sister, Roberta Damon."

We nodded and smiled. She invited us to sit in the chairs in front of her desk.

Carolyn continued, "Our mother died in 1935 and she is buried in the Carnegie Cemetery beside our grandparents. Only small grass markers to mark their graves. We need a large family marker with the right information on it. Our grandfather's stone says, 'Rev. R.K. McGregor' and gives the dates including the months and years of birth and death. Our grandmother's says, 'Mrs. R.K. McGregor.' It's as if she didn't even have a name of her own."

"Yes, unfortunately, that's the way it was back then. No one thought to include all the information about the wives."

"That's right, and on our own mother's stone it says, 'Keith McBride,' and it gives the year she was born and the year she died. With a name like that, who would even know it was a female? And someone might wonder why this person was buried beside the McGregors. It doesn't even make sense."

Mrs. Hackney was nodding. "Do you have the information you want written on the large stone?"

"Most of it. We've done the research and found our grandmother's name. We have her death certificate which gives her birth and death dates. The only thing we don't know about our mother is the month and day of her birth."

Martha Hackney pushed a large album over to us. "Look through this. You might see a stone you like. If you'll excuse me, I'll be back in a moment." She pushed her chair back and stood. We hardly noticed her departure, so eager were we to get to our task.

We thumbed through the album and soon agreed upon a simple, grey granite marker. We wanted to put McGREGOR on one side, and put the correct information about the three of them on the other.

Mrs. Hackney stepped back into the room. She had an old, thick, album in her arms. "I'm not supposed to show you this, but it might give you the information you need." She opened the book and laid it on her desk before us.

"Oh, dear God. It's Keith's death certificate." Carolyn and I had identical reactions. First, a quick, vocalized intake of breath. Then, we stared at each other, faces contorted, tears streaming. "Quick, look. Oh, here it is. She was born September 15, 1906."

"Look there. There it is. She was twenty-eight years and six months old to the day when she died." I put my finger on the information.

"It was Mrs. Joe Bristow who gave this information to the registrar." Carolyn spoke excitedly, "That would have been her sister. That was Orvilla."

I nodded. I was staring at the line that read "cause of

death." On one line someone had written "broncho pneumonia." The date of onset was March 8, 1935. On the next line down, there was a question "Other contributory causes of importance." I saw through my tears the words: "post partum hemorrhage," and the notation, "January, 1935"—my birth month and year. I was fifty-eight years old. I was conscious that I had already lived thirty years longer than my birth mother. I was excruciatingly conscious that she had given her life for mine. I had heard enough sermons on the atonement, the shed blood, the substitutionary sacrifice, to be struck to the heart.

"I gave my life for thee,
My precious blood I shed,
That thou mightst ransomed be
And quickened from the dead."

"Oh, my God. Oh, my God. Oh, my God." I heard my own voice as from a distance, saying it over and over again. "Oh, my God."

We ordered the marker, put down a deposit, thanked Martha Hackney, put on our sun glasses, and went back out to the car. "I don't know about you, but I could use a drink. Want to go find a cup of coffee?" We laughed shakily.

"I'd just as soon get our work done."

"Okay. Where to next?"

We went to the office of *The Carnegie Herald* and asked if they had copies of old issues of their paper from the twenties and thirties. We were informed that they existed and were kept in the archives of the Carnegie library. Off we went to find the library. It was housed in the building that serves as the community center. There we met Lillian Cotton, the city librarian.

"Yes, we have the back issues of the *Herald*. You'll have to be very careful in handling them, though. They are brittle and fragile."

"We'll be careful," we promised.

She took a shallow box from a high shelf, a huge rectangular container marked *Carnegie Herald*, 1920-1940. Surely, it would contain information we were seeking–any clue to our past. We took the lid off the box and carefully lifted out the sheets, brittle, and yellowed with age. We read of Don and Keith's wedding in the paper dated November 30, 1927, of Donald's birth, of Roberta's birth, of Keith's death. We could not find an announcement of Carolyn's birth. I told her she had been left on the doorstep by gypsies. We asked permission to photocopy the pertinent articles. Lillian Cotton was gracious to let us carry the material out of the library and to the nearest xerox machine.

RICHMOND–1993

I picked up the phone and dialed the number that would become so familiar in the next few years.

"Mrs. Anderson?"

"Yes?"

"It's Roberta." I had said those very words when I had stepped up on her porch in January. It seemed a lifetime ago. "Carolyn and I are thinking of coming back to Carnegie sometime soon. We want to come see you."

"Oh, yes, honey. You come on." We chatted inconsequentially, and then she said, "I have something I want to tell you, but I'll wait until you come. I'm afraid it might hurt your feelings."

"Tell me now. You're not going to hurt my feelings, no

matter what it is." I couldn't imagine what on earth she thought could bother me.

"Well, honey, when you were born, you had a birth defect."

"Really? What kind of defect?"

"Well, your forehead was mashed in on the right side, and it pooched out on the left side. When my friend–the one who owned the cow–when she saw you, she said, 'Oh, this poor little thing. Well, it's a good thing she's a girl because you can comb her hair down over her forehead.' She was a doctor's wife, and she knew how to mold the heads of newborn babies. I asked her about that and she said to me, she said, 'I can teach you how to do it, but this baby is six weeks old and it may not work on her.' Honey, I spent hours and hours molding and massaging your head. So, when you come back to Carnegie, I want to touch your face. My eyes are not so good anymore, and I couldn't see you well enough to tell when you were here."

I promised her she could touch my face. We chatted some more. I told her I'd let her know when we would be in town, and we hung up.

As soon as I hung up the phone, I thought of her hands on my head. Two events came to my mind with startling recognition. One was an EEG that the doctor had ordered months ago. I had been wired up across my scalp. They did the test, which went well. Afterwards, I sat up on the table and wept copiously. I was deeply embarrassed, and apologized to the nurse.

"I'm sorry. I don't know why I'm doing this. I can't stop crying. Where did this come from?"

"That's all right. People have different reactions to this. You'll be okay."

The other memory was the time my massage therapist, Tracy Gillespie, had massaged my head, and inexplicably, I had wept as she did her work. I never had known exactly why. I now believed that both incidents were connected to those events when I was six weeks old. The hours May Anderson had spent massaging and molding my head were coded into my memory bank. Both the EEG and the massage had triggered some deep and primal emotion in me. The body remembers. I thought of May's hands on my head. It was a blessing and a benediction.

CARNEGIE–1993

We went by to see Mrs. Anderson. The first thing I did was to put my face close to hers and put her hands on my face. Her gnarled fingers searched until they found and felt my forehead. "Not a sign of it." She smiled. "It's gone. Not a sign." She sat back in satisfaction.

I did not ask her about what my father must have thought when he first saw me. Perhaps she did not know. Did he think I was brain damaged? Did he believe I was going to die?

ALEXANDRIA, VIRGINIA–1948

When I was fourteen, daddy handed me a box full of his newspaper clippings. "Bertie, I want you to put these in some kind of order. You could paste them in this album." He gave me a black scrapbook with oversized manila pages. "They just need to be preserved for the family history."

"Sure, Daddy. I'll do it." I began sifting through and reading the clippings. I was proud that my daddy's name was in the paper: "Don McBride to head Oklahoma Water

Resources Board," "McBride to National Reclamation Association for Seventeen Western States," "McBride Appointed as Kerr's Legislative Assistant." I spread out the newspaper articles in a circle on the living room floor and sat in the middle of them. I placed them on the pages of the album in chronological order. It looked bland. I decided to spice up the album by borrowing a title from Ralph Edwards and his radio show: "DON MCBRIDE, THIS IS YOUR LIFE." I printed it on the title page in huge block letters. I asked my mother's permission to look through the box where she kept family photographs. I gathered pictures from daddy's early life–his parents, James and Lottie Belle Doyle McBride; daddy's baby picture; a picture of him as a Boy Scout; another of his eighth grade graduation; daddy, at twenty-four when he came to Oklahoma as a young engineer. Suddenly, I thought of my birth mother who had died.

"Daddy, what do you want me to do about Keith?" I looked up from the floor at him. He and mama were sitting on the living room couch. Mother tried to appear disinterested.

Daddy quickly responded, "Leave all that out. That's a closed chapter in my life. Just skip that part."

Mother looked pleased. I didn't argue.

CARNEGIE–1995

I promised Mrs. Anderson I would come to see her in the nursing home the next time I came to Oklahoma to visit friends and relatives. I arrived in mid-August. It was hotter than the hinges of hell. I was staying in Edmond with Wilbur and Gladys Lewis, old college friends. One morning, as Dr. Wilbur and I were sitting on the terrace, I told him in great detail the story of my discovery of Mrs. Anderson.

I said to him, "Wilbur, Mrs. Anderson told me she carried me home and took me off all the medication they had given me in the hospital. I asked her what was wrong with me and she told me I had blood poisoning–that I had an abscess on my knee."

He smiled and said, "I guess that means you have carried a scar on your knee all your life."

I was thunderstruck. "My gosh! I have never even thought about that."

"Well, you probably have a scar on your knee. Check it out."

I scrambled to roll up the right leg of my blue jeans. "Oh, my soul! There it is! It's little, but it's there!"

"We are fearfully and wonderfully made."

Dr. Wilbur insisted I take his car to Carnegie, and so I found myself behind the wheel of his Cadillac, on my way down the now familiar road. When I arrived, I decided to go by the florist and then to the cemetery to visit Keith's grave before I made my way to the nursing home.

I stepped out of blinding sunlight into the dimness of the florist shop to the sound of a tinkling bell. It was like stepping back in time. The shop was a large, high ceilinged room with creaking wooden floors and pierced tin tiles lining the walls. Old fashioned ceiling fans stirred the air. On display were silk flower arrangements in a variety of garish colors. I walked to the counter at the back of the shop and rang the small silver bell. A pretty young woman came out of the workroom with an inquiring look.

"Yes, may I help you?"

"Yes. Please. Do you have three red roses? My sister and brother could not be with me today, but I am on my way out to the cemetery to put flowers on our mother's grave. I just need three red roses—one from each of us."

"Do you want silk roses or real ones?"

"I want real ones if you have them."

"Almost no one puts real roses out in this heat, but I'll see what I can do." She opened the refrigerator door and pulled out a bucket containing tea roses—pink, yellow, orange, red. She chose the prettiest buds and said, "I hope these will be OK."

"Yes. Those are fine. I know they won't last long, but I do want the real ones."

She excused herself and stepped back into her workshop with my flowers. I browsed through the shop. When I came back to the counter, I saw cards on which messages could be written. I flipped through them and came upon one with a copy in miniature of an old familiar print of two Edwardian children, obviously frightened, crossing a rickety wooden bridge at night. Hovering over them, shielding them from danger, was a guardian angel. The picture reminded me of my sister and brother, the children who had lost their mother. Lord knows, they needed a guardian angel. So did we all. I took out my pen and wrote, "To Keith, Our dear young mother who loved her children, even unto death. We will never forget. All our love, Donald Keith, Carolyn, Roberta Sue."

The florist lady came back with my flowers. I couldn't believe what she had done with them. They were nestling on a palm leaf, arranged with baby's breath, wrapped in florist's green waxed tissue paper, tied with a red satin ribbon, and topped with a bow. "Oh, thank you. They are beautiful. I also want to buy this card. How much do I owe you?"

"Two dollars."

"Oh, surely not. Your labor is worth more than that."

"No. Two dollars. I won't take anymore than that."

I shook my head and gave her the money. "I will never forget your kindness. How can I ever thank you?"

"Come back to see me the next time you're in Carnegie."

I headed out to the cemetery. It was nine o'clock in the morning, and the sun was already baking hot. I found the second gate and the old cedar tree. I pulled up, parked in the roadway, and walked the few steps to the McGregor plot. I was glad for the shade of the tree and stood for a moment in that brutal August heat. Suddenly, my eyes were blinded by tears. I spoke aloud. "I love you, and I never knew you. You never held me. I never called you 'Mama.' I never looked into your face. I never saw your smile. You died for me. Thank you, Keith, my little mother. Thank you for my life."

I laid the roses on her stone. They were watered by my tears. There were three roses—one for each of her children—three—"In the name of the Father, and of the Son, and of the Holy Spirit." They were blood red. I knew they would soon be lifeless in the heat—never to fully bloom. I touched the baby's breath and breathed its fragrance—so fragile, so fleeting. My tears were for my mother, dead these sixty years. My tears were for my sister and for my brother who had loved her so, and whom she had so loved. My tears were for myself, bereft of her love.

ℂ

I washed and dried May's face gently and put a cool damp washcloth on her forehead. I was mindful that she had molded my misshapen forehead when I was six weeks old. I massaged her hands with lotion. As I did it, I knew these hands had tenderly cared for me when I was a baby. It was time for me to go. I hated to leave her. She was so tiny there in her bed. She needed to be in this nursing home. There was no way she could take care of herself now. Her eyes pled with me to stay.

"Don't go." Her voice was weak.

"I don't want to go, but I have to get back to Oklahoma City. I'll come again as soon as I can. What do you miss? What can I get for you?"

She smiled. "A fountain coke with lots of ice would be nice."

I gave her one last kiss and walked out of her room and out of the building to my car. I drove to the drugstore on Main Street. The lady behind the counter looked approachable.

"There is a sweet, elderly lady in the Carnegie Nursing Home. Her name is May Anderson. If I leave you twenty dollars, will you deliver a fountain coke to her every day?"

"Why, I think that could be arranged. You can buy a lot of cokes for twenty dollars."

We made the bargain.

When I left the drug store, I drove by May's house one more time. It stood empty. I got out of my car and went to the unkempt flower garden. I picked pink carnations, blue larkspur, and pink sweet peas. I folded the flowers into a cone of notebook paper. And when I got back to Richmond, I pressed them in waxed paper.

Donald and I went to her funeral. I asked her grandsons if I could speak a word. They were kind enough to allow me that honor. I stood behind the pulpit at First Baptist Church in Carnegie that day. I explained to the people that I was one of the babies that May Anderson had rescued.

"I owe her my life. The doctors said that I would die, but she would not allow that to happen. She cared for me when I was a small child. She prayed for me every day for the rest of her life. She knew me for the first two years of my life. I knew her for the last five years of hers. Someday, I will meet her in heaven, and we will catch up on all the lost time. I thank God for May Anderson. Oh, how she did love the little children."

As I went back to my place beside my brother, a young girl stood to sing. She couldn't have been more than twelve. I heard the most angelic voice singing simply,

"Jesus loves me this I know,
For the Bible tells me so.
Little ones to Him belong.
We are weak, but He is strong.
Yes, Jesus loves me. Yes, Jesus loves me, Yes, Jesus loves me.
The Bible tells me so."

It was the love of Jesus that sustained May all her life. She believed in it. She exemplified it. She shared it. God bless her memory.

Vonore, Tennessee–1996

I was visiting Uncle Paul in Vonore. I had a speaking engagement in Gatlinburg and as soon as I could break away, I drove my rental car down to Vonore to spend the night. I had to leave to catch a plane back to Richmond very early the next morning.

"Paul, I need to get on the road to the airport by six in the morning. What time do you get up?"

"Oh, I'm up drinking coffee by four-thirty."

"Good. I'll drink coffee with you and that will give me plenty of time to get to the airport."

I didn't need an alarm clock to wake up on time. I quickly got up and washed and dressed. I went into the kitchen where the coffee was on. My uncle and I sat across from each other in the black morning.

"Paul, I'm trying to get all the Pattersons straight. Tell me the names of your brothers and sisters. I know some of them, but I can't get them in order."

"Well, the oldest was Mack. You know, he disappeared when he was a young man. He just went off and never did go back home or let anyone know where he was. Then there was your mother, Mary Lou. After her, there was Lucy. That was another one that we lost track of. Then your Uncle Ray. His name was Raymond Allen Patterson, and of course, you know he went out to Oklahoma to farm when he was a young man and he met and married Jewel Chibon out there. The reason Ray went out to Oklahoma was because Uncle John and Aunt Jenny had gone out and Aunt Addie had married the Hicks boy, and they were out there. You know that Addie and Aunt Suze married brothers. But anyway, after Ray, there were three boys and all of them died: Frank, Virgil and Howard. They were all gone before I was born. I can't remember which one of them died of lockjaw. Then your Aunt Ann—Annie May—was next. I was the baby, except for the baby that died at birth when my mother died in childbirth when I was five."

"Now, go back to my daddy's brothers and sisters; there was Uncle Jeff. He married Aunt Alice. You remember going down to Uncle Jeff's for the family reunion when you were a little bitty girl. That's when you ate all those grapes off the grape arbor and got sick. Then there was Uncle Lon—he was a rounder—Aunt Cordie, Uncle Albert, Uncle John, Aunt Addie, Aunt Suze, Uncle Neil, Aunt Crease, and then my daddy—your granddaddy, Jake. Now, it was John and Addie that went out to homestead in Oklahoma real early. I never knew them because I wasn't born before they had already left. And then Ray went out and got him a wife and a farm. That was later. And then, your mama went out to live with Ray and to work in the hospital there in Carnegie. I went out there for Christmas one year to visit Ray. I must have been about sixteen. I rode the bus all the way out to Carnegie, Oklahoma from Tellico. I had never seen country so flat and so brown in my life. I was glad to get back home to the green hills of Tennessee, I'll tell you that's for sure."

I wrote as fast as I could and interrupted only for clarification. I hated to leave. Paul was my mother's boy. She was his mother from the time their mother died. I loved him from the time I first knew him when I was three. I never remembered a time Paul was not in my life.

On the plane, I took out my scribbled notes. I looked at the names. Some of them, I had never known, but I was connected to them through the stories my mother told me. Some were long dead before my birth. But, some I remembered. I must have been five the Sunday we went to Uncle Jeff's for that family reunion. Pattersons had come from Oklahoma back to Tellico for the party. Mother dressed me in the rose taffeta dress that Marjorie McLain had outgrown. I felt like a princess. Uncle Jeff's place was made to delight a child. It had an orchard with all kinds of fruit trees–apples, plums, cherries, and pears–and the grape arbor, loaded with heavy purple-black fruit. The cousins had the run of the place that day. By the time the fried chicken, ham and biscuits, cakes and pies were spread on the long tables under the elms, we children had eaten enough fruit to give us all a three day belly ache.

I remembered those women, probably in their fifties, with their hair skinned back into buns. They wore no makeup. Some of them had lost teeth. No one thought to do anything cosmetic. It was just a part of life to lose a tooth for every child born, to be old at fifty, to wear dresses clean, but unadorned, and Eleanor Roosevelt shoes. These women knew nothing of fashion, but they knew much of life.

I scanned the list of names. Aunt Addie—Addie Hicks. She and her husband had gone to Oklahoma as a newly married couple. Aunt Addie was one of the blonde Pattersons. My Grandmother Grace, who died long before my birth, was a blue-eyed blonde. Grace married my Granddaddy Patterson who had dark hair and olive skin. My great Aunt Addie and my Aunt Ann and my Uncle Paul were fair. They all had light hair, skin that burned in the sun, and blue eyes. Ann was a carbon copy of my great Aunt Addie—in color and build. Both women had small breasts and big hips. They were shorter than the brunettes. My mother and my Uncle Ray were tall and dark-haired with skin that would tan spectacularly if they so much as sat in the pale sunshine. They took after Grand-daddy Patterson. I didn't look like any of them, since I wasn't blood kin. I used to tell people that my mother never had any children. Ordinarily, that statement would elicit either a question or a very strange look.

I remembered going to Aunt Addie's house in Carnegie when I was a little girl, a stucco house the color of honey. Pressed into the stucco before it dried were tiny bits of colored glass—blue, the color of the glass jars Vick's Vaporub came in—bright red, amber, green, and clear. Every child who stepped up onto that porch thought it looked like a fairy castle. I remember trying to dig out some of the glass with my finger-nail. To my disappointment, I couldn't dislodge it. Aunt Addie churned her own butter long after other women quit. She had a garden with every flower known to God and man. Once, she gave me four o'clock seeds and mother let me plant them in our garden at home. I remember my mother said, "These will grow bushy and big. And the roots will go clear to China." I believed her.

Three houses down from Addie's was where Uncle John

and Aunt Jenny lived. I remember climbing up in their porch swing and listening as the adults talked. They were old, old people then—must have been sixty—who sat on the porch and talked and dipped snuff. I thought it was the nastiest stuff I'd ever seen. When Uncle John kissed me on the cheek, I saw his mustache stained with tobacco juice come toward my face, and I smelled the sick-sweet odor of it. I saw that my mother was pleased that I allowed his small attention to me. I liked Aunt Addie's house better.

Knoxville–1978

The phone rang in our Curitiba mission house. I answered and my brother's voice came across the five thousand miles. "Bert, I have some bad news. Dad is in a coma. They think he may have brain cancer."

"Oh, no. Please, not this."

"You'd better come on home. We are in Fort Wayne. Carolyn and all her family celebrated his birthday with a party. This morning, he fell down the stair to their basement. I got to see him before he lost consciousness. The doctors don't give us any hope."

"I'll be there as soon as I can get there."

By the time I could get out of Brazil, Donald had called me back to tell me that daddy was gone. I suddenly remembered the last time I had seen him. I had spent the month with him after mother's death just seven months ago. When it was time for me to go back to Brazil, daddy took me to the Knoxville airport, hugged me hard, and looked at me with the bluest eyes on earth. He spoke what turned out to be his last words to me. "I love you, honey." And then, he had fled. Now my brother was calling to tell me he was gone. We agreed that I would meet Carolyn and Donald in Knoxville at daddy's house. I was stunned. Bill saw me off in Curitiba. It was beginning to be an old story.

When I walked into mom's kitchen in Knoxville, before I had a chance to put my suitcase down, Carolyn said to me, "I don't want you here. Don and I could have taken care of everything without you."

I looked at her through red-rimmed eyes. "He was my father, too, Carolyn."

Friends were in the house. Carolyn was telling how daddy had come to Fort Wayne. She had met him at one of the shops. She drove him to her house, stopping on the way to buy some rose clippers at the hardware store. All her children had been at the house for their grandfather's birthday party. She described the cake. She went into great detail. When another friend would come in, she would go through the story again for the fresh audience. I began to feel sick at my stomach. All the McBride brothers, our uncles, came in for the funeral. Del Ray friends were there from Virginia. It was like living again the funeral for mother seven months earlier. At least it was June, and it was not raining.

Finally, the funeral was over. I walked down the driveway to dad's mailbox and pulled out two notes. Both were from people in the neighborhood. One was from a young mother. Her note said that dad had been kind to her and to her children. He had always stopped his yard work to chat with her whenever she was out pushing her babies in their stroller. He had known the names of her children and always inquired about her family. She had written, "It may seem a small thing, but I wanted to know that your father was kind to me and I shall miss him." The other note said, "If you are going to have an estate sale, call me first at_____," and gave a phone number. With what emotion I had left over from the anxiety and sorrow, I was furious. I went back into the house and shared the two notes with Don and Carolyn. They were moved by the first and outraged by the second.

We were sitting in mother and daddy's den. This was the day we buried our daddy. I felt unreal.

Carolyn was telling me something. "So, when Donald and I were in Knoxville to spend time with daddy–the time we fixed his sidewalk in the front of the house–I went to him and I said, 'Donna is the only granddaughter you have. I know mother gave Roberta $20,000 because she's a missionary. So, I want mother's crystal and china and sterling, and I also want her big diamond. I think that's only fair.' So daddy said to me that he would do it. And he said that the only reason he and mother had given you the extra $20,000 was because Bill would never provide adequately for you. I asked him to put it in writing, and he did."

Before I left Brazil to go to daddy's funeral, I had said to Bill, "Mother and daddy left me about $20,000 more than they left Donald and Carolyn. I want you to know, just to nip any ill feelings in the bud, I'm going to divide it three ways." Bill nodded. "Anything you want to do is fine with me."

Now, we three sat and made our plans for the next day. Suddenly, Carolyn said to me, "Do you want me to tell you what daddy really thought of Mark?"

"Not unless it's really loving. I don't think I could bear to hear criticism of my child right now."

"Well, he thought Mark was lazy and would never amount to anything."

"Carolyn, please. Not now."

"Well, mother may have always loved you best, but that's

okay because daddy always loved me best, so it evens out."

I got up from my dad's big rocking chair and walked blindly out to the garage, found a pair of daddy's work overalls, and cried silently into them. Oh, Carolyn, must you do this?

The next day, we went down to the bank and divided the extra money our parents had left me. It was money well spent. Then, we dismantled the house. Our dad had left us a letter asking that we not fight over material possessions and admonished us to love each other:

"Love each other for our sakes. Don't drift apart. Be concerned for each other. Pray for each other. Trust God, and remember that your mother and I always prayed every day for each of you. I hope one day that we will be together in heaven and our Lord can say 'Well done.' I thank God for her, and for her being your mother. She loved you and me. I love you.

With love,

Your Dad."

We agreed that we would not bicker.

As Carolyn loaded her car with mother's Haviland china, the Rose Point sterling silver by Wallace, and the Heisy "Moonglow" crystal, I kept reminding myself, "It's just stuff." The only discordant note that day was within me. I had not one regret about dividing my money three ways, but I did have some uncharitable thoughts when my sister packed up mother's things. It wasn't even that I wanted my mother's treasures. It wasn't that I didn't want her to have them. It just seemed so ironic and wrong, somehow, that Carolyn was packing up all the beautiful things in the light of the fact that she had spent most of her life despising mother. Her dislike obviously did not extend to what mother had owned and treasured.

We divided furniture by choosing pieces in turn. I chose pieces I wanted to keep, but also pieces Sarah Ann and her mom had requested. I gave Grandmother Patterson's crystal fruit bowl to our Aunt Ann for safekeeping. I told her to put my name on it. It had been on mother's dining room table for as long as I could remember. But, I thought Ann should have it. After all, it had belonged to the mother she had lost so long ago when Ann was a little girl.

I watched Carolyn pack her car. I thought there couldn't possibly be room for one more thing. Eleanor Brockenridge from San Antonio, Texas, who founded the Texas Woman's Suffrage Association in 1913, left a wonderful quote. Why did my mind repeat it over and over as I watched our family scene? "Foolish modesty lags behind while brazen impudence goes forth and eats the pudding." Ah, well. It's only stuff. I could not recall one day in my life that I missed a meal because I didn't have the money to buy food. I could not recall ever sleeping out in the cold because I didn't have a bed or a roof. How much is enough? What is need and what is greed?

Carolyn drove back to Florida. I went home with Don to spend a few days with him and Mary, and then he took me to BWI for my flight back to Curitiba. Bill and the children were glad to see me. It was good to be home.

$\mathcal{R}$ICHMOND–1997

At four, Melissa, our dear grandchild, asked me one day, "Mimi, are you old?"

"Yes, honey, I am."

"How old are you?"

"I'm sixty-four years old."

"Are you sick?"

"No, I'm not sick."

"Are you going to die?"

"Yes. One day I will."

"But I love you. I don't want you to die."

I scooped her up in my arms and hugged her. "Melissa, you don't have to worry about that. That's God's business. God will take care of me. And God will take care of you." She seemed content.

ALEXANDRIA, VIRGINIA–1951

I don't know if daddy had an affair. I suppose he did. I do know that he and mother had some discussion about divorce. One reason I was sent to Oklahoma that summer, I suspect, was so that I could avoid the marital discord. The day I was packing for my trip, out of the blue, mother asked me, "If your father and I got a divorce, would you want to live with him or me?"

My heart contracted sharply. "You, Mama, of course." What kind of a question was that? If daddy had asked me, I would have assured him that I wanted to be with him.

Then, when daddy and I were alone together in the car, he said to me in an aggrieved voice, "My secretary called your mother and told her I was in love with a woman who works in our office building. She said that every morning I came in saying I was going upstairs to get my daily inspiration from Mary. Can you believe that? I know there are some men who go wild over any woman who flips her skirts at them, but I would certainly not do anything like that. I certainly would not. Certainly not."

I remember that I felt, even at sixteen, that my father "doth protest too much, methinks." One "certainly not" would have sufficed. What was going on here?

Sometime at the end of that summer, mother said to me, "Your father asked me what I would do if he ever decided to ask me for a divorce."

"Why would he ask you a thing like that?"

"I don't know, but I told him I would give him a divorce, if that's what he wanted, but I would take him for every dime he ever thought about making. I pointed out to him in no uncertain terms that I gave up a career as a surgical nurse to marry him. I have been faithful to him. And I have scrubbed his floors, cooked his meals, and single-handedly taken care of his kids for all these years. No judge in his right mind would rule in favor of him and his paramour."

"What did he say?"

"He said, 'That's what I thought you would say.' And he hasn't mentioned it again. I don't think he will."

Life settled back into a routine. As far as I knew, there was no more talk of divorce, or of daddy's marital dissatisfaction, or of his being in love with someone else. I have no idea what happened to the other woman in question. I'm sure she went on with her life. People rarely die for love. I was relieved that I was no longer pulled between my parents—at least overtly. I loved them both and feared them both. I did not want to be forced to choose one over the other. I was sixteen and had about as much on my plate as I could handle. I didn't want to be required to hate daddy for his betrayal or to rescue mother because of her pain. Thank God, it was over.

I doubt that mother ever forgave daddy completely. I know she never forgot. Years later, after his prostate surgery, he told her that God was punishing him. I found it interesting that he believed that God chose to disconnect the apparatus that had been the instrument of so much of daddy's sinning. There was a lot of superstition in that belief–a departure from grace, a throwback to the dictum that "God's gonna getcha." One day during our furlough year–the year mother was terminally ill with a heart condition, she said to me, "I will say this once, and then we will never speak of it again. I deserve what I got. If I was fool enough to marry Don McBride, God gave me just exactly what I deserve. Now, we will not speak of this again." She obviously felt that she had it figured out. I didn't feel I should try to argue her out of it. I stood helpless before her pain. This time, I was not sixteen, but forty-one. I still couldn't make life right for her.

*T*he Years–1935-1993

I didn't dare love Keith. My security was tied up with Mary Lou. I harbored some atavistic belief that if I displeased her, I would lose her. I heard the story over and over. The one about the time I said of Keith to Mary Lou, "Don't worry, Mama, I didn't know that other woman anyway." With the repeating, the adults would laugh, taking the comment as proof that I was untouched by the death of my birth mother–that Mary Lou was my true mother, and Keith was irrelevant.

I remember stories about the McGregors, always told in a negative light—how our grandparents would bring presents to Donald and Carolyn and would bring nothing for me. The story was told of the time I toddled across the kitchen floor and Grandmother McGregor said, "There goes Keith's life." Did I really remember the event, or had I heard someone tell it, and I only thought I remembered? No. I remembered. I remember the linoleum and the angle of the rays of light coming in the kitchen window. I remember how the light spilled onto the floor. Ann once told me, "Your parents (referring to Daddy and Keith) weren't getting along." I remembered Mary Lou saying that "Poor Don would go spend time with Harry Jolly in the evenings, because he hated going home to the chaos. His dinner was not ready, and the children were wild." She also told me that both Grandmother and Granddaddy McGregor had "mental problems." I remember hearing about how the McGregors would take Carolyn and Donald to the cemetery where our mother was buried, and everyone would cry. By the time I was old enough to know anything, I understood on some elemental level that I was not to love my birth mother. No one said it out loud. They didn't have to say it. I was not to ask questions about Keith. I was to be loyal to Mary Lou and love her exclusively. This I did with all my heart.

When I was twenty-four, and expecting our first child, a woman came up to me in Northwest Baptist Church in Oklahoma City where Bill was youth minister. She said, "I grew up in Carnegie. I knew Keith McGregor, your birth mother. She was wonderful." I remember literally cutting the woman off and walking away. I did not want to hear about Keith. I did not want to talk about her. To do so would have been a disloyalty to Mary Lou.

When, at age thirty, I wrote my autobiographical material for our Foreign Mission Board in view of our appointment for overseas service, I was highly defensive of Mary Lou. I wrote: "I strongly suspect I was an unplanned blessing. My mother, Keith McGregor, daughter of a Baptist preacher, presented my father with me. My mother, who was very beautiful and not very stable emotionally, lived through the delivery and survived until March when she died as a result of my birth." Where did I get the idea that my birth mother was not very stable emotionally? It probably came from the stories that Mary Lou and Ann told me. The prevailing belief was that all the McGregors were crazy. They told me that Grandmother McGregor used to hide in the basement in a trunk until Granddaddy would call the police. Everything would be in an uproar until they found her. In my autobiography, I described Mary Lou as "capable, intelligent, and emotionally mature." I continued, "By the end of the year, my dad was in love with her. She had become indispensable to us all. The smartest thing my daddy ever did was to marry Mary Lou Patterson." That may have been true, but why, at age thirty, did I still have a need to believe Keith was crazy and Mary Lou was a saint? Maybe it was because I had lost two mothers already, although at the time I was unaware of the existence of May Anderson. Maybe I was still terrified of losing my mother. Maybe, in an effort to please her, I joined in denigrating the McGregors. Carolyn was not the only one in the family who needed to be loved exclusively. Mary Lou needed that kind of love from me. "Love me, love me, and no one else. Love me best." There didn't seem to be enough love to go around. It was some kind of rationed commodity.

Mary Lou was a powerful figure in my life. She was influential in every decision I ever made—which school I would attend, what subjects I would study, which boys I dated, whom I married. I always weighed those decisions against her opinion, her approval, her disapproval. I broke up with a sweet young man to please her. There was nothing wrong with him, but he was going to be a chemist. Years after, I spoke with his mother. I told her that Mary Lou had said that I could never be happy if I married her son. She responded, "Yes, and she would have made sure of it." Ah, Mother! Later,

I broke an engagement to please her. That young man was going to be an attorney. Mother was looking for a missionary.

Much later, although mother never questioned my calling, I certainly did. Finally, I wondered if I was called to be a missionary to please her. She spoke with the voice of God. After all, she had seen the Presence. "But Mary (Lou) kept all these things and pondered them in her heart." What would any of us do if God came into our room the very night a child was born? Would we not assume the responsibility of molding that child into, at the very least, a candidate for missionary service? When I allowed myself to be angry with her, I felt better, until the guilt kicked in.

Once, for therapeutic purposes, I jotted all the reasons I "should" be angry with my parents.

1. Daddy was going to give me away by letting the Andersons adopt me.

2. Daddy forgot about me.

3. Daddy and Mary Lou lied to me.

4. They didn't tell me about Mrs. Anderson.

5. They had "big sins" they were hiding while being very religious.

6. They let me be their sacrificial lamb.

7. They programmed me to be a missionary never allowing me to look at another career or marry anyone who had another career.

8. I was robbed of a relationship with Carolyn and Donald.

9. I was robbed of a relationship with Mrs. Anderson.

10. I never got to know Mr. Anderson or Charles.

In 1981, after we had come back to the States from Brazil, I was in graduate school at Southwestern Baptist Theological Seminary, in Fort Worth, working toward a degree in marriage and family therapy. Students were encouraged to attend the annual meeting of the Texas Association for Marriage and Family Therapy. That January it was held in Galveston. On Sunday morning, when all good Baptists were in church, I stayed for the last day of the conference. The Flagship Inn had been turned into one big conference center. Not only were the regular conference rooms in use, but what were usually guest rooms had been stripped of beds and furnished with folding chairs. Informal small groups of workshops and seminars were scattered throughout the complex. I squeezed in to what was formerly a bedroom. Several presenters shared what they had just completed in the way of research in academia.

Most of the presentations that day were based on doctoral dissertations soon to be published in scholarly journals. One woman had done a study on vocational choice and parental influence. I found her study applicable to my life. She had interviewed nuns and had found some interesting correlations. Her thesis was that many nuns choose religious vocation in order to please their parents. The nuns were the "good girls." They would get the family into heaven.

As I listened to her, I felt uncomfortable, flushed. Suddenly, a memory came sharply into focus. I remembered that my sister had flung an accusation at me. "Miss Goody Two Shoes, you became a missionary for one reason, and that was to please mother and daddy." I remembered the gut-wrenching anxiety I had felt at her barb. I remembered my defensive and adamant denials. Now, I was open to hearing of the possibility. Parental influence is, after all, a powerful force. Why did I think I was immune?

I have long since accepted as fact that I was programmed from very early to be a missionary. Was it God's plan? Was it my mother's plan? What difference does it make? We did some good work in Brazil. It was a time of growth and joy, and anguish, and pain—like life. Do I regret the almost twenty years we spent there? No. Do I want to go back? No. Do I want to be sixteen again, or twenty, or thirty-five? No. No. No. If I have learned anything about "God's will," I have learned that life gives us choices. One choice might be right for a time. Doors close. Other doors open. I learned that after we came back to the States, one of my older relatives expressed disappointment that I had turned my back on God's will for my life. Perhaps my mother would have felt the same way. She was so proud to say that her daughter was a missionary. But what a strange view of life to believe that "God's will" boxes us into such narrowly defined roles.

I was a prisoner of my mother's love for me. And my love for her was real and deep. I owed her a huge debt. Sometimes, I paid dearly. Her obvious disapproval could send me into paroxysms of self-doubt. Mother really did know best. When she died, I thought I would die, too.

Among those who study families, it is a well accepted fact that when a parent becomes enmeshed emotionally with a child, the family configuration is skewed. The relationship between husband and wife must be primary. When a child becomes surrogate spouse to a parent, the family can only be called unhealthy. This is not to imply any sexual misconduct. It is, however, a kind of emotional incest.

My mother began early to get her emotional needs met from children. She always had a favorite. First it was her little brother, Paul, to whom she was a mother. Then, she loved me best. After that, she was partial to Sarah Ann, Paul's daughter. Later, she chose Kathy, Ann's daughter. In her last years, she was partial to our son, Mark. In some ways, she considered all of these children the ones who needed rescuing. She loved and mentored three generations of children. In so doing, she certainly loved and taught them. She also sought to meet her own emotional needs from them. My father did not know much about meeting the emotional needs of his wives, or his children. He had abdicated long ago. One of the difficulties of choosing one child over the others is that, invariably, there were those who were not chosen. Carolyn and Donald felt that rejection most deeply.

Life is so seldom simple. Saintliness and selfishness can so easily dwell within the same troubled breast. And what we believe about our mothers at thirty is often not at all what we know at sixty-five. Wisdom does not automatically come with age, but if it comes at all, it comes late. There is, of course, the wisdom of childhood, but that is often naivete–innocence, mistaken for wisdom–just as some virtue is nothing more than lack of opportunity. Mature wisdom comes out of life experience. If I have learned anything, it is that there is enough love to go around. Love is never rationed. Loving one does not mean stealing love from another

$\mathcal{W}$OMEN'S MAGAZINE QUESTIONNAIRE

$\mathcal{I}$f your mother died at your birth, you will need professional help to enable you to process." I heard a therapist say those words in a seminar, years ago. At the time, I did not believe him. I honestly believed myself to be unaffected by Keith's death. Soon after, I was leafing through a women's magazine while I was under the dryer at my hair salon. I saw an article entitled, "If Your Mother Died at Your Birth," with a questionnaire attached. I couldn't tear the article out, nor could I filch the magazine, so I reached for a pencil and scribbled the ten questions on a half sheet of notebook paper. Later that day, I went back and jotted my answers.

1. As a child, did you ever feel responsible for your mother's death? Yes.

2. As you look back, do you feel people tried to shield you from the idea you were responsible for her death? Yes, Mary Lou and Ann defended me.

3. Did anyone ever say in your presence if it weren't for little Johnny, Helen would still be alive? Yes, Grandmother McGregor.

4. Did you ever in your life go through a time of grieving for her? When? What age? No, I was not allowed, nor did I think it necessary.

5. Did your father remarry? Yes.

6. How did you relate to your stepmother? She is the only mother I have ever known. We get along very well. I love her very much.

7. Were you taken to your mother's grave as a child? Never.

8. Have you since visited her grave? No.

9. Do you think her death affected you in the way you act and react? (Do you strive for acceptance, drive yourself, feel yourself to be unworthy?) I strive for acceptance. I have always driven myself. I have been afraid, but never have I felt unworthy.

10. Did her death affect your choice of vocation or spouse? No.

Later, as I read back over my answers in that earlier time, I marvel at my denial, and my lack of self knowledge. It is incredible to me that as long as Mary Lou was living, I did not grieve for Keith. I did not believe I had the right. It is incredible that it never occurred to me to want to visit Keith's grave. And, of course, both my choice of a husband and my choice of a career, were intertwined with my mother's death and all the subsequent family history. An event as cataclysmic as my mother's dying in childbirth could not but affect and shape my life.

I do remember once, when I was fifteen, I asked daddy, "My first mother didn't die as a result of my birth, did she? Didn't she die of pneumonia?"

My father heard the question, but did not understand what I needed to hear. He said, "Oh, no. She died because of your birth. She bled to death. I remember the doctor calling me in and telling me to put all my weight on her belly. Her blood ran down the leg of the table she was on and it pooled on the floor."

"Oh."

RICHMOND–2001

When I was very small, I learned a prayer at church:
"Thank You for the world so sweet.
Thank You for the food we eat.
Thank You for the birds that sing.
Thank You, God, for everything. Amen."

When it was my turn to offer grace at mealtime, that would be the prayer I would repeat. In our family, it was recognized as my prayer. Years later, in the beginning stages of my seminary career, I studied early childhood education. Rote prayers were frowned upon as being unworthy. "We should teach children to pray from their hearts and in their own words," said my professor. There are days, now that I am old, when my back yard has been washed by early morning rain, and the cardinals are at the feeders. Then, I pray that childish prayer again. And it comes from my heart.

My brother has often wondered what his life might have been had his Granddaddy McGregor been around longer to help him through the teen years. Certainly, he wonders what life would have been like had Keith lived. He was marked by the deaths of the two people who nurtured him. Over the years, he developed a cordial and loving relationship with mother and daddy. It is a truism that we all need to forgive our parents, but I have always believed that true forgiveness takes place when the offender asks to be forgiven. "I know what I did wrong. I _____. I know what I failed to do. I didn't _____. I should have_____. I'm sorry. Please forgive me. Let's have a better relationship in the future." Never, in a million years, would it have occurred to our parents that they were at fault, nor would they have felt any need to ask for forgiveness. I doubt that either Mother or Daddy would have seen themselves as parents who had failed. In their early view, Donald was a stubborn and difficult kid who went his own way and made a mess of his life. In their early view, Carolyn was simply impossible. That my brother could say "I love you, Mother," while she was dying, and mean it, borders on the miraculous. I don't know when Donald began to love our parents, or when they began to love him. But love happened.

By the time Donald had established a relationship with our parents, he had finished high school and earned a college degree on the G.I. bill. He went on to complete a Master's in sociology. Who said he was stupid and lazy? Neither Donald nor Carolyn was ever encouraged to get an education. However, Donald chose to take advantage of Uncle Sam's offer to pay for his schooling. He came late to value education. Carolyn never pursued her education beyond junior college. She had a good mind, and could have become anything she might have wanted. Instead, she blamed our parents for not encouraging her—a part of her victimization.

Donald, like our father, married three times—once at eighteen without a clue about life, once immediately after the first divorce, and, once after he had grown up. At the age of forty-eight, Donald retired from the Social Security Administration after thirty years with the federal government. Then, he became a printer.

Carolyn, too, finally experienced love and approval from our parents. In the last two years of mother's life, Carolyn made a concerted effort to court them. She showered them with little gifts–funny things she had picked up at craft shows–small lounging ceramic frogs, a corkscrew apparatus to dip in honey, a feather duster. She dropped in unannounced. She sent packages with dried apricots and shelled pecans with notes saying, "Pretend it's Christmas," or "Pretend it's your birthday." Mother and daddy were delighted with the attention. But, like her truce with me, it was not permanent. At their deaths, the old resentment toward me bubbled. By the time the three of us decided to spend some time together to make up for all the lost time, the old pain and anger toward them returned as well.

The Fourth of July of 1980, two years after daddy's death, Donald and I drove to Fort Wayne to spend two days with Carolyn. She had managed to plan it for a time when her family was busy elsewhere. The three of us sat and ate and talked and laughed and drank coffee. We had a wonderful visit. Then Bill and I invited Carolyn and Bob and Don and Mary to our house for Christmas that year. Somehow, all our grown children were off doing other things. We ate Christmas dinner and opened our gifts and sat by the fire. It was quiet and restful.

Carolyn and I were together rarely, but when we were, everything kicked into high gear. "Let's sponge paint a border around the guest bedroom ceiling." "Let's go buy tile and put a splash guard behind your kitchen sink." "Take me to a place I can get these prints framed." "I need to go by a craft store and see if I can match this yarn." Wherever she went, Carolyn left her mark. Everyone in the family had quilts, crafts, and throws that she had made by hand. The gifts were great. They were made during her manic phases when she neither slept nor ate. I discovered I could take about three days of my sister, and then I needed to go back to real life.

Donald and I made several trips to see Carolyn when it could be "just us three." There would be much raucous laughter, outrageous comments, and then, inevitably, the talk would turn to our childhood, the old pain, sorrow, and inequity. Carolyn had a need to repeat her litany over and over again. It was not that she had never seen a therapist. She had seen many over the years. She would engage a counselor and tell about her deprivation and victimization. The therapists would listen sympathetically. When they began to suggest ways for her to get beyond the past, she would find another therapist and start all over again. Therapy "never worked."

I never heard my father say the words, "I'm sorry." He would be sorry. He would do things to make up for what he had done wrong, but to my knowledge, he never uttered the words. Once when our boys, Mark and Paul were little, we were visiting mom and dad in Knoxville. The children had their toys scattered across the den floor. When dad came home from work, he took one look at the disarranged room and yelled, "Look at this mess! You kids get in here and clean this up and I mean right this minute! I've never seen any worse kids than you two! You get busy and I mean right now! When you're at my house, you will not behave like this!" He turned to me, "People hate to see you coming with these two brats!" In that instant, I became a frightened child. The three of us jumped up and began picking up toys. My children were white-faced with fear. So intimidated was I by my father, I felt helpless to defend them. The next day, he gave them quarters. My mother said that was his way of saying "I'm sorry." I needed to hear the words. "I'm sorry," is sometimes sweeter than "I love you." It was not until the last year or so of my father's life, when I had acquired some self confidence, that I was able to counter his attacks. I began to forthrightly disagree with him. I learned I would not die if my opinion were contrary to his. Nor would he. My mother, now frail and fragile, told me, "I just love the way you stand up to your father." I thought a moment and said, "Me, too."

My dad was so human—not wicked or evil—just human. He had a terrible temper, which he never bothered to curb. His temper only subsided over the years with his dwindling testosterone levels. When that happened, he mellowed. People in the family would say, "Isn't it wonderful how much nicer he has become. He has learned to control his temper."

Years ago I was at an American Association for Marriage and Family Therapists (AAMFT) meeting in Chicago. I attended a video presentation in the huge ballroom of the Sheraton where perhaps five hundred marriage and family therapists attended the session. The video was a documentary of a twelve-step group meeting. A man who had been an active alcoholic for years had sobered up and had become an evangelist, preaching sobriety. He said to the support group he was addressing, "People come up to me all the time and tell me what a changed person I am. It's great to live sober. I am a changed man. This life I am living now beats hell out of the one I was living." Everyone in the group "high-fived" him. The man's wife was also in the group. She allowed him to tell of his metamorphosis, and then, she spoke to him and to the group. "It is truly wonderful that you are now clean and sober. I'm glad you are. Life is better now by far, but we have been married for twenty-five years. For the first twenty one of those, you were drinking. Let me tell you how that was for me. I never knew when or if you were coming home. When you did come home, I never knew if you would be drunk or sober. I never knew if there would be money for groceries, or if the water or phone would be cut off because you didn't pay the bills. When the phone rang, I never knew which creditor would be on the line threatening me with legal action. I never knew when you would go into a blind rage. I never knew when you would throw things and break things. I never knew when you were going to beat me or the children. I lived in hell. Our children lived in hell. With the money you spent on booze, we could have lived like kings. You would like to believe the first twenty-one years don't count. I just want to say one thing to you. They count." The five hundred therapists sitting in that ballroom burst into loud applause.

My father was thoughtless, and thoughtful. He was selfish, and generous. He was serious, and he was funny. He was self-absorbed, and concerned. He was bright, and dumb as dirt. Daddy was not an easy person. Although mother craved serenity, daddy created chaos. Daddy married mom and then, went off to conquer the world. She did the child rearing—not always sweetly or even willingly, but she did the major work of it. She cooked and cleaned and remained faithful. Daddy flirted and patted. He may have had an affair. He had horrendous secrets in his past. He lost his temper and verbally abused all of us. He physically abused the children. He never said, "I'm sorry." Not once.

At the end of his life, dad was nicer than he was before. After his death, we were going through his papers. I found two little blue memo sheets from his office in Knoxville. He had written a note about mother. It was addressed to no one. It read:

"If you want to know: there is no escaping the

fact that my wife, Mary Lou, deserves more of the credit for any success I may have had than I do. It was she who had the judgment that kept me on track. And she had a faith that was contagious. I never made a public appearance or a speech that I was not very much aware of her prayers for me at every crucial moment. When I would have a desire to exhibit pride (which was too often), she would always remind me to "walk humbly," and to thank the Lord for an opportunity to serve a proper cause. She would ask if there was a possibility that words of praise may have been out of courtesy instead of from the heart. Yet, without undue fuss, she let me know she was proud of the acclaim I received.

So, if anyone takes the time and effort to dig through these files, for whatever purpose, I hope you will know that my beloved wife was indeed my partner for which I am humbly grateful and very proud."

I sighed. This was his way of saying "I'm sorry." I remember my mother's saying, "Your daddy can be nice to me at home, but he will wait until he gets me out in public to insult me." It reminded me of the comedian who was doing his monologue on stage. There was a heckler in the audience who was giving him a hard time. After the show, both the comedian and the heckler found themselves in the men's room. The heckler looked at the comedian and said,

"I'm really sorry I heckled you. I know I made it really tough for you. I want to apologize to you."

"That's okay," answered the comedian. "Next time, though, I would like for you to heckle me in the men's room and be nice to me in public."

I sighed again as I folded the blue memo paper with daddy's note. I thought, "Oh, Daddy. I just wish you could have been this nice all the time."

Richmond–1999

Donna, my sister's only daughter, pulled the book out of her tote bag. "I brought this to you. I have my mother's cookbook and I know how much it means to me. I thought you should have this."

"Oh, Donna. How can I ever thank you? I grew up seeing Mary Lou use this. I can remember where she kept it in the kitchen. Look, she clipped recipes and pasted them all through this. Here's the one for Cherry Winks. She made those cookies every Christmas for as long as I can remember. My goodness, that was the winner for the second grand national Pillsbury bake off. I have no idea what year that was."

"Look, here's that lemon-pineapple Jello salad she always fixed for company. Good heavens, it has vinegar in it." We sifted through the clippings she had collected over the years.

"Oh, look at this. "Mrs. Johnson's Lemon Cake and Bess Truman's Special Brownies. Here's Jacqueline Kennedy's Tuiles–whatever they are. Some of these mother never made, but some of these she used over and over."

Donna turned back to the front cover. "Look at the inscription: 'Mrs. Don McBride' and the date '11/24/27.' I wonder if that's Keith's writing?"

"No. I think someone gave her this as a wedding gift.

That's the date of her marriage to your grandfather. Her writing is here on the inside front cover. Look how Mary Lou pasted recipes over it. And here's Mary Lou's handwriting. Here she wrote 'Mrs. Don McBride.' It's like the inscriptions on those old tombstones. Women's names became the names of the men they married. So many of them died without a voice—without an identity of their own. It's sad to think that while men were writing laws, composing symphonies, governing, and building empires, women were cooking their food, and birthing and tending to their babies—and, of course, dying in childbirth. You have to wonder what women might have been able to accomplish on a grand scale if they had been given the opportunity. Of course, some of them did great things, but they were in the minority. Women's roles were so narrow, and the work they did was so temporary—weaving and spinning, cleaning and childcare, sewing and cooking. Their work absorbed all their time and energy, but it was impermanent, and once it was done, it needed to be done again and again.

"Donna, thank you for this cookbook. What a gift! You are dear to give it to me. I will treasure it for the rest of my life."

When Donna left, I sat for a long time with the book on my lap. I smiled over some things. I recognized Ann's handwriting. She had written out a recipe for Lazy Daisy Cake. There were recipes from Ruby Ryan and Jessie Lovelace—two of mother's good Del Ray friends from her Alexandria days. There was the recipe for Aunt Bill's Brown Candy. Mother had made that candy—a blonde fudge—every Christmas in my memory. That recipe was printed in the Oklahoma City newspaper in December of 1942—the year I was seven. The thought of Aunt Bill's candy still makes my mouth water. Mother had clipped that recipe and had neglected to trim some fillers.

One declared that bunions are caused by lack of Vitamin A. Just beneath was a blurb entitled "Buy War Bonds." The entire article consisted of one sentence: "Don't be a 10 percent war bond housewife if you can be a 15 or 20 percent one." I assume housewives were urged to buy bonds with ten percent or more of their household money.

Years of memories came flooding back to me–the family around the dinner table at six o'clock every night–no matter what was happening emotionally, we knew the food would be plentiful and excellent. I remember the huge crock on the back porch where mother made her own sauerkraut. I remembered the time daddy brought in a Rush Springs watermelon and said it must have weighed fifty pounds. He put it down and picked me up and said, "I think you weigh as much as that watermelon." I thought of all the holiday meals–the hams and turkeys and all the dressing and gravy, the sweet potatoes in orange shells, pumpkin pies made from scratch and cranberry relish in the white bowl. I remembered that my brother's favorite dessert was banana pudding. I remembered the Sunday dinners when company came. I remembered mother at the stove on Sunday morning putting the roast on before we went to church. All through the years, the visiting preachers during weeks of revival, would eat at least one meal at our house. The "girls" in mother's Sunday School classes came for Bible study and dessert.

There is no one else in the world, now, who cares about this book. It is, after all, not holy writ. To me, though, it is sacred. This is heilsgeschicte—that German word I learned in David Kirkpatrick's systematic theology class so many years ago–heilsgeschicte. It means "holy history," referring to God's breaking into human history with the covenant, the promise, the chosen people, the incarnation, the atonement. My story is as old as Genesis. It, too, contains all the pain, the mistakes, the passion, the tears, the forgiveness and the lack of it, the anger, the anguish, and the joy. My story is of sin and promise, shed blood and redemption. Perhaps, after all, it, too, is holy history. I took up my pen to write.

"To Melissa Rebecca Damon:

This cookbook was presented as a wedding gift to my birth mother, Keith McGregor McBride, November 24, 1927. She died at the age of twenty eight as a result of my birth in 1935. The book was used for many years by my stepmother, Mary Lou Patterson McBride. She died in 1977 at the age of seventy four. My sister, Carolyn McBride Brown then took it as a keepsake. When Carolyn died April 6, 1999, it went to her daughter, Donna Brown, who gave it to me as a gift, in remembrance of my two mothers who used this book. Since I have no daughters except by marriage, I pass it on to you. You are the next girl in this long line. Keep it, my dear child, in tender memory of the grandmother who loves you so dearly, and in honor of those strong women who went before. Love is stronger than death.

Mimi"

The first time I ever heard the expression in Brazil, "*coracao de mae*," I laughed. Some of our seminary students were piling into our car. Someone murmured, "*coracao de mae.*" It means "a mother's heart," and the implication is that there is always room for one more. I find that I have room in my heart for all three of my mothers: Keith, so young and tender; May, so kind and dear; Mary Lou, so protective, and determined. My heart expands to include them all.

I thank my mothers for their legacy of faith. I envision

them together in heaven, arm-in-arm, like three tough, battle-scarred veterans. God's own hand has wiped away all tears from their eyes. "And there is no night there. They need no candle, neither light of the sun, for the Lord God gives them light." They look upon the very face of God. "And there is no more death, neither sorrow nor crying. Neither is there any more pain." No more do they weep for their children. And they shall reign forever and ever.

Love is stronger than death.

AFTERWORD

CARNEGIE–AUGUST 17, 2002

Why are we pulled back again and again to this place? To these graves? To the memory of these women? Why was the mother of three small children taken at the age of twenty-eight, while another was given a span of ninety-five years? Why was one woman barren, desperately wanting a child, while another was fecund and warned not to bear again?

This day, we stood at the graves of both Keith and May. We thought of Mary Lou, dead these twenty-five years. Incredibly, two of my three mothers are buried in the same cemetery. The other lies far away on a hillside in Tennessee. Today, we knelt and wept and embraced in sorrow and gratitude. Love and pain and history bind us all, bringing us into the circle of shared humanity.

Roberta M. Damon, author, *A Voice Beyond Weeping*
Gladys Lewis; original editor and publisher

If you're a Fan of this Book, Will You Help Spread the Word?

www.robertadamon.me

There are several ways you can help me get the word out about the message of this book...

- Post a 5-Star review on Amazon.

- Write about the book on your Facebook, Twitter, Instagram—any social media you regularly use!

- If you blog, consider referencing the book, or publishing an excerpt from the book with a link back to my website. You have my permission to do this as long as you provide proper credit and backlinks.

- Recommend the book to friends—word-of-mouth is still the most effective form of advertising.

- Purchase additional copies to give away as gifts. You can do that by going to my website at: www.robertadamon.me

The best way to connect with me is at: www.robertadamon.me OR P.O. Box 3402, Chester, VA 23831

ENJOY THESE OTHER BOOKS BY ROBERTA DAMON

Theirs is the Kingdom: A Fictionalized History of the Early Christian Church

Power – Politics – Romance – Intrigue – Faith
Roberta Damon skillfully blends historical facts and characters to create a masterful, inspiring and educational read!

Dear Mrs. Noah: Letters to Unnamed Women of the Bible

There are many Biblical women whose stories are known, but whose names are not recorded. Roberta Damon writes letters to 34 of these women, gives them appropriate names, and grants them new identity.

Dear Abishag: Letters to Little Known Women of the Bible

These 30 women have something to say to you...
Tucked within the pages of Scripture are little-known jewels—stories of women whose lives have something to say to us today.
These are their stories. Use these compelling letters as a daily devotion to build your faith and renew your hope.

You can order these books from

or where ever you purchase your favorite books. You can also order these books from my website at: www.robertadamon.me

NEED A SPEAKER FOR YOUR NEXT PROGRAM?

Invite me to speak to your group or ministry. I have forty years of public speaking experience. If you would like to have me come speak to your group or at an upcoming event, please contact me at: www.robertadamon.me OR P.O. Box 3402, Chester, VA 23831

COMMENTS FROM PARTICIPANTS:

"A breath of fresh air."
"I could listen to her all day."
"Come back again. We loved hearing you."
"I loved your story."

POSSIBLE TOPICS

- Women in the Bible
- Marriage and Family
- Grief
- Depression
- Identity Issues
- Family of Origin—including my own story